MONTEREY PENINSULA'S

SPORTING HERITAGE

RANGERS ABALONE CUP JUNE 30 1930

Through the 1920s and the Depression years that followed, baseball was America's game. In avant-garde Carmel, the Abalone League version was softball and required each team to field two female players. Here the Rangers pose in June 1930 at the Carmel Woods venue off Carpenter Street.

FRONT COVER: This is John Gardiner, coach of the 1948 Big Green Shirt football team at Monterey High School and later tennis professional and owner of John Gardiner's Tennis Ranches. (Courtesy Dan Albert.)

COVER BACKGROUND: The photograph captures a part of one of Charlie Frost's Bomber baseball teams. It was taken at the old ballpark in Monterey. The year was 1943, and the country was in the middle of the Second World War. (Author's collection.)

BACK COVER: Six pals and the dog pose at the high school football field in Monterey during the war. (Author's collection.)

MONTEREY PENINSULA'S
SPORTING HERITAGE

John W. Frost

ARCADIA
PUBLISHING

Published by Arcadia Publishing
Charleston SC, Chicago IL, Portsmouth NH, San Francisco CA

Printed in the United States of America

Library of Congress Catalog Card Number: 2007933018

For all general information contact Arcadia Publishing at:
Telephone 843-853-2070
Fax 843-853-0044
E-mail sales@arcadiapublishing.com
For customer service and orders:
Toll-Free 1-888-313-2665

Visit us on the Internet at www.arcadiapublishing.com

This book is dedicated to Charlie Frost, who gave and gave to a generation of Monterey Peninsula kids. One of them is shown standing in center field at the old ballpark on Franklin and Adams Streets. It was built in 1928 and demolished in 1954. The landmark aluminum-coated PG&E tanks loom up from where the Monterey Sports Center now stands.

CONTENTS

ACKNOWLEDGMENTS

Thanks to my wife, Helenka, who graciously gave over our living room for several months to the clutter of my research and writing. Dr. John Castagna guided me and my photographs through the scanning process while becoming a friend, and I cannot thank him enough. Along the way, I came to appreciate Arcadia's formatting and its friendly interpretation by Devon Weston. The archivist at the Monterey Public Library, Dennis Copeland, was extremely helpful during my usage of the material at the California History Room Archives. I am also grateful for the time and assistance given me by Jim Conway, museum coordinator and historian for the City of Monterey, Tim Thomas of the Monterey Maritime History Museum, Faye Messinger at the Mayo Hayes O'Donnell Museum, and Rose McLendon at the Local History Room of the Harrison Memorial Library in Carmel. Thanks, as well, to Todd Buller, assistant principal at Pacific Grove High School.

Most of my photographs came from old friends who entrusted me with their memories, knowing that I was doing it for all of us. I thank Jim deLorimier, Gloria Avila, Donn Hare, Pat and Darold Sunkler, Dan Albert, Virginia Albert, Louise Cutino, Jack Holt, Mrs. Richard Collins (Sheila), Bob and Marian Woodward, Lawrence Segovia, Sal Russo, Gretchen Bartowick, Sally Schuman, Gertrude Woods, Larry and Doris Matthews, Kathryn Alkire, Don Prince, Felix Spiegler, Lawson Little, Doug Forzani, Sal and Mary Jane Colletto, Sal Cardinalli, Bill Askew, Bob Miyamoto, Don Davison, Sheryl Mueller, Owen Greenan, Ray Cardinale, Russ Bohlke, Mike Marron, Frank Flores, Luke Phillips, and Colin Kuster. I wish to extend a particular word of gratitude to Jim and Therese Hare and to Gene and Joan Vandervort for including me in their monthly luncheons.

Several people gave useful advice or assistance at the right time, and I am thus indebted to Ann Clark, Sue Blois, Edie Karas, Cameron Bianchi, Don Butts, Katy Miller, Joe Morgan, Kent Seavey, and Court Stewart, and I especially thank local legend Tom Enea for sharing his encyclopedic knowledge of Monterey sports history. Images with no credit line are from the author's personal collection.

INTRODUCTION

The towns of Monterey, Carmel, and Pacific Grove, and what is in between, constitute the Monterey Peninsula. It was a magical place to grow up and to live out one's life in the early decades of the last century. There was the rugged coastline and the protected bay, the white-sand beaches and the gnarled cypresses, and gold, grassy hills spotted with oak trees in the valleys of the interior. The explorer Viscaino had grasped its beauty centuries before and claimed it for the king of Spain. Much later, Monterey became the capital of California, and not long after, in 1880, Charles Crocker opened the luxurious Hotel Del Monte, offering socialites and dignitaries an array of activities to go with the natural beauty of the area. The hotel put up appropriate facilities along the contiguous beaches of the bay and built its own polo field and track for horse racing. There were lawn tennis courts, a warmed saltwater pool, horse-drawn carriages for exploring a 17-mile drive around the peninsula, and just before the dawn of the 20th century, the hotel laid out its own golf course.

In 1915, the Crocker family and its Pacific Improvement Company liquidated their real estate holdings, including extensive property on the Monterey Peninsula. Carrying out this task for them was S. F. B. Morse, an ex-Yale footballer and distant relative of the inventor of the telegraph. Having demonstrated his business acumen in a couple of other projects in California, Morse, endowed with foresight and Fleishhacker financing, purchased the Monterey Peninsula property for himself and formed the Del Monte Properties Company to develop it. Golf was the centerpiece of his real estate vision, and within a decade, Morse had built two of the finest courses in the world, Pebble Beach Golf Links and Cypress Point, to add to the one at Del Monte. A fourth course, at the family-oriented Monterey Peninsula Country Club, opened in 1925, and a fifth was developed in cooperation with the City of Pacific Grove in 1932.

From the inception of its golf course in 1897, the Hotel Del Monte hosted important events, and Morse built on that tradition at his new Pebble Beach Links. During the moribund 1930s, while the company struggled financially, Morse maintained his vision of a recreational empire that would be unmatched anywhere in the world. When the war was over, he heeded the advice of a local journalist and brought the Bing Crosby Pro-Am golf tournament to the peninsula, showcasing his two already legendary courses as well as the Dunes Course of the Monterey Peninsula Country Club.

In his promotion of the sporting possibilities on the peninsula, Morse revived polo in the 1920s, an activity that had begun to wane with the advent of the automobile. He became a forceful member of the state polo association and encouraged the polo greats of the day to bring their ponies in for the season at Del Monte. In the doldrums of the Depression, polo participation once again flagged, and during the war, the Del Monte fields and racetrack were taken over by the navy. However, there were over 100 miles of bridle paths in the Del Monte Forest, and when Morse built the Pebble Beach Lodge and Golf Links in 1919, he had the perspicacity to add an equestrian center for the use of the buyers of his real estate. After the war, the center blossomed and became internationally known in the hands of Dick Collins.

The hub of tennis activity in Morse's empire remained at the Hotel Del Monte through the 1930s, and many of the great players in the country performed there. When the hotel was taken over by the navy in the war years, tennis moved over to Pebble Beach. In 1949, John Gardiner was lured from Monterey High School, bringing with him Jack Frost, an already nationally prominent junior player, thereby attracting attention to Pebble Beach tennis.

Sam Morse's empire thrived on tourism, enticing people to the peninsula to stay at the hostelries and play his public course at Pebble Beach and consequently buy real estate. Of the local communities, both enchanting Carmel and sleepy Pacific Grove, with its spectacular drive along the water, fell splendidly within Morse's vision. There was only one irritant in "Happy Valley." It was the Monterey fishing industry, which had begun slowly in the 1890s with Japanese abalone divers and remained relatively small even after the first fish cannery was established in 1902. Soon enough, however, it was discovered that the world wanted sardines, and by 1920, there were 9 canneries, and a decade later there were 30. The sardine fishing and canning industry, like most else, declined during the 1930s, and just after the war, sardines disappeared from the bay.

As a competitive man, Sam Morse had resented an industry that was at least the size of his own. He did not like the fishy odor that permeated everything when the canneries were running and the ethnicity behind it. He did what he could to block its expansion. Yet much of the service labor Morse needed to run his empire came from the Monterey side. For example, the part of town called Oak Grove, to the east of Lake El Estero, was settled largely by employees of the large Hotel Del Monte laundry. Their kids caddied at the hotel's golf course and worked the canneries, too. Generally, the Monterey Sicilian kids who caddied gravitated to Pebble Beach and the Spanish ones from New Monterey carried bags at Cypress Point.

Added to the working-class nature of their existence, the two major immigrant groups in Monterey, the Sicilians and the Japanese, were of old-country backgrounds that were insular and secretive. They found their expression in the world of sports, which for the Sicilians, especially, meant baseball and football. The Japanese also were very active in the major sports both at the public schools and through their culture club next to the ballpark.

As a rule, residents of Carmel and Pacific Grove had easy access to Sam Morse's empire, insofar as their incomes would permit, while one is hard-pressed to find any Italian, Japanese, or Spanish names among the membership rolls at the Del Monte clubs over the first half-century. The upshot was a Monterey swagger that arose out of a sense of social inferiority, a "don't come over the hill" attitude toward its Carmel and Pebble Beach neighbors and a particular intensity toward its high school sports. Some of the fellows from those Monterey days still meet every morning for coffee and discuss such matters. The photographs seen in this book are almost all from the scrapbooks of these people, as well from the golfers, tennis players, and riding enthusiasts who inhabited Sam Morse's recreational empire. They are from Carmel and Pacific Grove, from Salinas families and Carmel Valley cowboys who came from just outside to enhance the sports heritage of the Monterey Peninsula. These photographs are not likely to be seen anywhere else. It is the hope that this book does justice to the memories.

1

BASEBALL

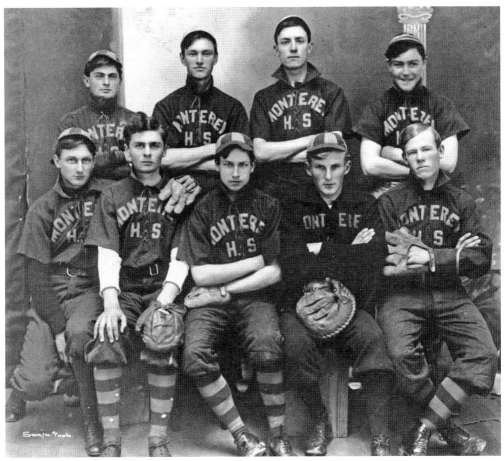

The Del Monte and Monterey Union High School opened for classes in August 1904 on the top floor of the wooden grammar school at 700 Pacific Street. There were 35 students with a faculty of seven to serve a town of roughly 5,000 people. In 1909, the name was changed to Monterey County High School and finally to Monterey Union High School three years after that. Monterey joined the Coast Counties Athletic League and won the baseball championship in 1909 with a team comprised largely of the players seen here. Chester Hare, seated fourth from the left, son of county surveyor Lou Hare, served on the school's board of trustees for several years in the 1930s. He was responsible for lighting being installed on the football field for night games. One of his sons, Jim, became a legendary athlete at Carmel High School, and a grandson, Steve Hare, was head football coach there in the 1960s. (Courtesy Donn Hare.)

In 1892, Fr. Ramon Mestres, pastor of the San Carlos Church in Monterey, seeking a place for his young parishioners to play organized baseball, paid $150 for a year's lease on a wheat field owned by David Jacks. The plot, not far from the church, was bordered by Figueroa, Franklin, Pearl, and Adams Streets. The ground was leveled, a fence built, and a grandstand raised. It became the home of Father Mestres's San Carlos Cadets, who competed against Catholic boys' teams

from the Santa Clara Valley and elsewhere. It also was used by the town team, whose games were enjoyed by locals as well as guests of the Hotel Del Monte. The event depicted here took place in September 1922. (Courtesy Monterey Public Library, California History Room Archives; photograph by A. C. Heidrick.)

One young fellow to cut his teeth on the Monterey ball field was Harry Wolter, who went on to coach the Stanford University baseball team for 26 years; another was Carmel Martin (left), who was reared on the Martin Ranch—later the Mission Ranch—in Carmel. He went to Colton Hall School, which is now the city hall in Monterey. Eventually Martin graduated from the University of Michigan, where he pitched on Big 10–title teams in 1905 and 1906. Returning to Monterey, he was soon elected mayor and served as a member of the board of trustees of the high school for 23 years. Monterey High, with its present campus dedicated in 1915, continued to play baseball at the downtown field. Shown below is the 1923 team. (Left, courtesy Bob Miyamoto; below, courtesy Pat Sunkler.)

BASEBALL

Hal Youngman was born in Perry, Missouri, to a circuit-riding preacher and his wife. The itinerant family wound up in Southern California and Hal Youngman at Pomona College, where he is shown in 1913 with his block "P" and decked out for baseball. He came to Monterey High in 1927 as coach of all varsity and lightweight sports, and when he left 20 years later, he had earned legendary status. (Courtesy Sheryl Youngman Mueller.)

An organization of baseball enthusiasts in the 1920s, led by John Meehan and calling itself the "Stickers," pressured the City of Monterey to build a proper ballpark. The new facility was dedicated with great ceremony in 1928. This 1930 photograph looks toward home plate. In the middle of the group is hard-nosed catcher Jim Drake, whose two daughters became touring softball players 20 years later. (Courtesy Marian Drake Woodward.)

In putting up the new ballpark in 1928, the city fathers of Monterey anticipated its use as a spring-training facility for the San Francisco Seals. In the opening-day exhibition game, the celebrated Lefty O'Doul, who loved the Monterey Peninsula and its golf courses, played for the town nine against the Seals, whom he was later to manage for many years in San Francisco. (Courtesy Monterey Public Library, California History Room Archives.)

Carmel incorporated in 1916 with a population of 638, and beginning in 1921 through the mid-1930s, its athletic highlight was Abalone League softball. During its peak years, eight teams competed; each team had 10 players, two of whom had to be female. At first, they played at Carmel Point and later in the Carmel Woods off Carpenter Street. (Courtesy Harrison Memorial Library, Local History Room.)

The 1930 Abalone League Shamrocks pose at the Carmel Woods venue. Pictured from left to right (first row) are Monterey High School athlete Sis Reimer and Lucy Marsh; (second row) Carmel apothecary Doc Staniford and writer Tal Josselyn; (third row) World War I aviator and developer Byington Ford, Frenchie Murphy, unidentified, Charlie Frost, Dr. Paul Hunter, and Harold Geyer.

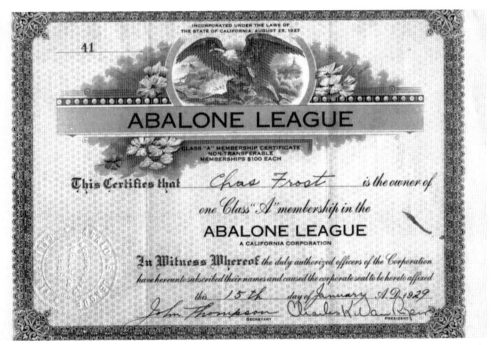

With Carmel flair, the Abalone League purchased the Arts and Crafts Theatre on Monte Verde in 1927 in order to stage its own plays and to produce an annual "Abalone Follies." At season's end, an awards banquet was held at the Hotel La Playa, with the champion team receiving a stovetop that had been purloined from the *Monterey Herald* newsroom. In 1929, shares were issued to help finance the league's activities.

In Pacific Grove, girls had been playing softball at the high school since at least 1909, but it was not until 1932 that the city, with Works Progress Administration (WPA) and private funding, put up a proper municipal ballpark. It was located on 17-Mile Drive near Pico and has since been known locally as "Pico Park." Shown here is the 1923 Pacific Grove High girls' softball team. (Courtesy Pacific Grove High School.)

Japanese immigrants began to come to the Monterey Peninsula in the 1890s, mostly to dive or wade for abalone. They created a large settlement, clustered around the site where the ballpark was to be built in 1928. Their principal social and educational center was the Japanese American Citizens League Hall at 424 Adams Street, across the street from the entrance to the ballpark. (Courtesy Monterey Public Library, California History Room Archives.)

Schools at the Japanese American Citizens League (JACL) Hall and at the Japanese Church on Pearl Street opened in 1927, offering language and broader cultural instruction, including martial arts. By 1936, two teachers taught 85 children at the hall and a single teacher instructed another 75 of varying ages at the church. At Monterey High School, the Japanese Club met once a month and by 1938 had 50 members. (Courtesy Monterey Public Library, California History Room Archives.)

Paralleling instruction at the JACL Hall was the formation of a sports organization around 1927 that came to be known as the Minato Athletic Club. Within a few years, Minato baseball teams were winning statewide championships. Pictured here is the 1935 squad, from left to right: (first row) Bob Sakamoto, Roy Hattori, Mas Higashi, Yoneo Gota, and Jim Takigawa; (second row, in uniform) Yo Tabata, Ky Miyamoto, Kaz Oka, Archie Miyamoto, Jim Tabata, and Haruo Esaki. (Courtesy Monterey Public Library, California History Room Archives.)

Ky Miyamoto, from the class of 1934, was one of the finest athletes ever to graduate from Monterey High School. His long-jump record stood for three decades. When he was asked to join the Nisei Alameda Kono all-star team on a baseball tour of Japan and Manchuria in 1937, he eagerly accepted. Here a few of the players are seen warming up on the way over. (Courtesy Bob Miyamoto.)

The *Chichibu Mara* departed San Francisco in early March 1937 for Yokohama via Honolulu. She returned in late July. The team, assembled on board for this photograph, from left to right, are (first row) Sadamune and Mirikitani; (second row) Nushida, Yano, Yamada, Enimura, Kono, Iwahashi, Takaki, Ishida, Tukumoto, and Nogami; (third row) Allisen, Alleruzo, Riggs, Davis, Kawakami, Suzuki, Tanizawa, Hiramatsu, and Miyamoto. (Courtesy Bob Miyamoto.)

BASEBALL

The Japanese empire was expanding in Asia, and it had annexed Manchuria. The tour there took the American team to Mukden, Port Arthur, and Dairen. In Japan proper, they were at Beppu Springs and Moji in Kyushu and on the island of Shikoku, and on Honshu, they played in Osaka, Kyoto, and Tokyo. The American team and their Japanese counterparts meet during pregame ceremonies in traditional fashion at home plate. (Courtesy Bob Miyamoto.)

Baseball was introduced to Japan in the 1870s, and by the 1930s, it was the second most popular sport after sumo wrestling. For several years, beginning in 1931, Lefty O'Doul went over annually to play exhibition tours and took with him the biggest names in American baseball: Babe Ruth, Lou Gehrig, Jimmy Foxx, and others. They performed at the ballpark in Osaka, as did Monterey's Ky Miyamoto and the Kono All-Stars. (Courtesy Bob Miyamoto.)

Ky Miyamoto's father, Kumahiko Miyamoto, came to Monterey from Japan in 1900. He married a Japanese-born woman whose family had settled in Shell Beach. Together they farmed on the Martin Ranch in Carmel and are credited with having brought artichokes to the area. Here Ky Miyamoto (left), while on tour, visits some of his mother's family and a paternal uncle (in black robe). (Courtesy Bob Miyamoto.)

Congregated on the field at Hiroshima in 1937 are, from left to right, Ky Miyamoto (Monterey), Shiro Kawakami (?), Mas Yano (Fresno), Al Sadamune (Alameda), Charles Hiramatsu (Guadalupe), Kiyo Nogami (Alameda), secretary Pop Kubota (Tokyo), Ben Tanizawa (Alameda), and Ed Suzuki (Honolulu). Eight years later, the ballpark and the entire city of Hiroshima were to go up in a mushroom cloud of atomic destruction. (Courtesy Bob Miyamoto.)

The close-knit Miyamoto family had been dispersed during World War II. Ky Miyamoto, who had spent a year at San Jose State University before touring Japan with an all-star baseball team, enlisted in the U.S. Army. He was assigned to the *Nisei* 442nd, which was ordered to Fort Howze, Texas, on the Oklahoma border. He spent much of 1943–1944 as a medic there, taking advantage of what athletic opportunities he could. In the above photograph, he is fifth from left in the second row with an assembled group of ball players; at right, he and a "Reception Center" teammate pose playfully for the camera. Following the war, Miyamoto pitched virtually unhittable softball for the Carmel Pine Cone team and played basketball for the Frost Roofers until he was close to 40 years of age. (Courtesy Bob Miyamoto.)

As the peninsula pulled out of the depths of the Depression, athletic possibilities expanded accordingly. The Monterey ballpark was the site of this kids' baseball jamboree in the late 1930s. Architect Bob Stanton financed one of the teams, and Monterey city councilman Charlie Frost, at the far left in the third row, was just beginning to involve himself with kids' baseball. Standing to the right of Frost is Mayor Emmet McMenamin, and fifth from the left is Jeff Jeffries, who brought a group of young African American players over from the Salinas area. A few years later, Jeffries would apply his generosity and enthusiasm to organizing sports at Bay View School in New Monterey. At the far right of the third row is Goldie Goldstein, who worked for years as a bailiff in the sheriff's department and played on the town team in the mid-1930s with the Ventimiglia brothers, Derby Minafo, John Baptista, Phil Calabrese, Cookie Vargas, and Frank Cefalu.

BASEBALL

One of Charlie Frost's wartime Bomber baseball teams is pictured by the first-base dugout of the ballpark. They are, from left to right, (first row) Jack Frost, Vince Maiorana, Nick Marotta, Tom Incaviglia, Tuxedo, and Lou Frost; (second row) John Bevilacqua, Sal Colletto, Junior Balesteri, Tom Russo, Bob Toole, George Toole, Jack Schaeffer, and Pvt. Snuffy Snith; (third row) Charlie Frost, Tony Aiello, Bill Wardle, Frank Mercurio, Bart DiMaggio, and unidentified.

Monterey chief of police Fred Moore was an advisor to the boys' club, attended all the important games, and sometimes came to practices. Here he would have been offering a few pregame words to a small but loyal c. 1943 wartime crowd seated in the bleachers behind home plate.

This was the Frost Bomber team (above) from the summer of 1943. Pictured from left to right are (first row) Jack Frost, Jiggs Ward, Roy Robertson, and Vince Maiorana; (second row) Marty Larkin, Jim Grammatico, Sal Cardinale, Edgar Williams, Daryl Sanchez, John Bevilacqua, and Don Day; (third row) Jerry Blanchard, Tom Incaviglia, Sal Colletto, Bob Toole, two unidentified, Bill Wardle, Jim deLorimier, Lou Frost, Bart DiMaggio, and Charlie Frost. Toole, Day, Larkin, and deLorimier were from Pacific Grove and typified Charlie Frost's effort to bring together kids from the three towns with varied backgrounds as friends in the sports arena. In a similar vein, pitcher deLorimier (left), seen at left with catcher Bevilacqua, recalls playing twilight softball games the summer before at Pico Park in Pacific Grove against soldiers from the African American 54th Coast Artillery Regiment, which was stationed at nearby Point Pinos. (Left, courtesy Jim deLorimier.)

The 1944 Bomber team formed the nucleus of the later Monterey High School squad of 1947, with John Buceti, Tom Incaviglia, and Pete Bartowick doing the pitching, which won its first CCAL championship in 20 years. Pictured here from left to right, they are (first row) Tom Perez, Incaviglia, Sal Colletto, Tom Russo, John Bevilacqua, and Bob Toole; (second row) Jim deLorimier, Buceti, Frank Mercurio, Al Click, Lou Frost, and Richard Lee.

Charlie Frost paid all the expenses for his kids' teams, arranged their games, and ran their daily practices. They played twice at Seals Stadium in San Francisco; he drove them up in the back of his truck, and they had lunch at the Carnation Creamery. Bob Toole, seen here, was the first baseman. His son later starred at shortstop for Santa Clara University.

At left is Tom Incaviglia, whose son, Pete, spent a decade in the major leagues. At right is Bob Toole, next to his mother, who was cut from the same cloth as Hilda Chester, the Brooklyn Dodgers fan who attended every home game at Ebbets Field in the late 1940s and razzed the umpires mercilessly. In the local version, Mrs. Toole's target was usually the forbearing Andy Del Monte, a Carmel policeman who worked behind the plate at most of the kids' games.

Charlie Frost fielded a Junior Bomber squad, which is shown here. Pictured from left to right are (first row) Roy Childress, Laurence Segovia, Bob Marron (batboy), Vince Ruiz, Jack Frost, Jim Jones, Tom Enea, and Stony Bruno; (second row) Sal Cardinalli (whose parents can be seen in the stands behind), Mike Marron, Al Earl, Carmel Martin, Daryl Sanchez, Joe Grammatico, Vince Bevilacqua, and Joe Kirby. Earl was active in San Francisco baseball circles and 35 years prior had caught Martin in semipro ball.

A popular baseball venue, particularly for younger kids, was the Monterey High School football field. A group of pals are at the gridiron in 1943. Pictured from left to right are Jack Frost, Mike Marron, Edgar Williams, Tuxedo the dog, Gene Roncarati, John Douglas, and Junior Martorella. During World War II, an obstacle course for military training was set up around the perimeter of the field, elements of which can be seen in the background.

In January 1943, there was a huge turnout for Charlie Frost Day at the Monterey High School stadium. Four years later, an appreciation ceremony was held at the boys' club on Polk Street at which John Cardinale (right), president of the club, presented an inscribed wristwatch to Frost.

Organized sports for females were slow to gain a foothold in Monterey. In 1917, girls at the high school were offered a "physical culture" class, in which they were taught "proper breathing, carriage, and gracefulness." It was not until Hester Schoeninger and Eudora Mitchell (Estep) came to the school in 1934 as instructors that girls were given more serious encouragement. Meanwhile, in Pacific Grove, girls' sports had been alive since the early 1900s, and in Carmel, a tradition of women in competition was built into Abalone League softball in the 1920s. The Carmel Youth Center girls' softball squad of 1946 consisted of, from left to right, (first row) ball girl Shirley De Amaral; (second row) coach Bonnie Giles, Eleanor Taggert, Jerry Yoakum, Joan Sanders, June Updike, Carol Templeman, Carol Ann Snith, and Carol Petty; (third row) Cynthis Zarafonites, Donna Douglas, Jackie Briggs, Dici Douglas, Diane Lewis, Jean Halett, and coach Jack Giles. (Courtesy Joan Sanders Vandervort.)

BASEBALL

Softball goes back to the roots of the peninsula's baseball culture, although the game was not known as "softball" until the 1920s. Pictured here are members of the 1940 Del Monte Spaulding softball team, from left to right: (first row) Lefty DeSoto and Jim Hodgen; (second row) Orrin Ford, Lefty Davison, unidentified, Mannie Chappel, and Sherman Beggerstaff. Chappel had been a standout member of Monterey High School's 1938 football team. (Courtesy Don Davison.)

Softball activity thrived on the peninsula after the war. Pictured here are members of the Grove Creamery team, from left to right: (first row) Frank Garnero, Secondo Maschio, Nick Albert, and Dan Albert; (second row) John Thacker, Doug Pottharst, Chet Garnero, Frank Thacker, and Bill Thacker. Frank Thacker became head golf professional at Del Monte and later at Spyglass. (Courtesy Virginia Albert.)

Marian Drake was president of the Girls Athletic Association at Monterey High School in 1952, and her sister Janet was the secretary. Yet it had become apparent that their softball skills far transcended what the school had to offer, and they were approached by Ruby Roberts, who ran the bowling alley on Pacific and Franklin Streets, to join her touring team. Ruby's Rockets traveled and competed throughout the state and into Oregon, with Roberts and Marian Drake doing the pitching and Janet Drake in the outfield. Their father, Jim Drake, caught against the San Francisco Seals during their spring training in Monterey 20 years earlier, and their cousin Merle Drake became a legendary softball pitcher, once having whipped the famous touring team known as the King and His Court. Ruby Roberts's championship Rockets of 1950 included, from left to right, (first row) Barbara Espinosa (bat girl), Delores Eddington, Marian Veramontes, Ginger Ramey, Helen Locicero, Norma Nelson, and Lilian Peart; (second row) JoAnn Knowles, Beverly Costa, Vivian Simmons, manager Joe Espinosa, Ruby Roberts, Betty Bomarito, Janet Drake, and Marian Drake. (Courtesy Marian Drake Woodward.)

BASEBALL

With travel restraints having been removed, recreational and professional baseball blossomed in the aftermath of World War II. The Western Meat entrant in the Mission League came out on top in 1946 and again in 1947 with a record of 31-4. Clarence Truesdell, the team's business manager, had been around peninsula baseball for years, while John Canepa and John Baptista played for the town team before the war. Lefty Davison had been too small to make an athletic impression at Pacific Grove High in the early 1930s, but later he became one of the fine ballplayers in the area. His son, Don, followed a similar path, as he went unrecognized at Monterey High but became a truly outstanding performer in basketball and baseball league play through the 1950s and 1960s. George Galios, the Western Meat catcher, was also one of the best golfers on the peninsula. Pictured here are members of one of the championship Western Meat teams. They are, from left to right, (first row) batboy Bud Henny; (second row) ? Truesdell, Jerry Bernstein, Jerry Devlin, Chet Garnero, Bob Henny, Galios, and manager Irv Henny; (third row) Lefty Davison, Canepa, Baptista, Ray Casas, Jack Riordan, Tom Ludico, and Arden Ardaiz. (Courtesy Don Davison.)

Walter Schulken was a promoter and a sports enthusiast who sponsored Monterey athletic teams in the 1950s. One of his finest hours was a game that he organized between a pick-up team of local youngsters and a similar group from the Los Angeles area. To heighten interest in the event, he promised to fly in "hundreds of celebrities." In fact, he produced "Beans" Riordan, the ex–Pacific Coast League umpire, and old "Foghorn" Murphy, who, in the days prior to public address systems in the Coast League, was employed to ride out to home plate seated on a donkey and bellow out the starting lineups. The game was won by the home team, decided by Laurence Segovia and Jim Stewart home-runs. Pictured is the Monterey side, from left to right: (first row) Joe Cardinalli, Frank Casas, Joe Rogers, Segovia, Dominick Mineo, Ray Cardinale, and pitcher Leroy Wentz; (second row) ? DeSilva, Murphy, Mike Artellan, Vince Ruiz, Biff Russo, Dale DeSilva, Barney Belleci, Sal Aiello, Dan Douglas, Stewart, Bob Napoli, Stony Bruno, Schulken, and Goldie Goldstein. (Courtesy Ray Cardinale.)

2

FOOTBALL

Pacific Grove's high school was dedicated in 1911. Monterey's came four years later, while Carmel, with a much smaller population, was not to have its own high school and campus until 1941. Over the first few years, Monterey failed to field a football team for want of "enough stout fellows," but in 1922, they played Pacific Grove and lost, and a rivalry began that was to endure through the 1930s. The Monterey yearbook, *El Susurro*, at one point referred to the football contest between the two schools as the "little-big game." In 1923, with a graduating class of 29 students, Monterey turned the tables on the Breakers of Pacific Grove. In this photograph, the 1923 Monterey squad is shown with the cement bleachers and school buildings as a backdrop. A science wing to the right and a new gymnasium to the left, both out of view, had been added the year before. (Courtesy Pat Armstrong Sunkler.)

LIGHT WEIGHT FOOTBALL TEAM MONTEREY UNION HIGH Nov. 1928

Coach Hal Youngman was hired at Monterey High School in 1927. In the previous year, the Green and Gold football varsity had gone winless, but in Youngman's first season, the team won the Coast Counties Athletic League (CCAL) B Division championship by scoring an upset victory over rival Pacific Grove. This was accomplished amid Breaker charges of ineligibility against redoubtable Monterey halfback George Parker, who was to earn five letters in each of his four high school years. Youngman achieved his remarkable turnaround by installing a double-wing formation and by conducting his first week of practices not allowing a ball on the field in order to teach blocking and tackling. Of course there were Parker and three other fine backs—Clyde Klaumann, Gordon Campbell, and Louis Davidson—to move the ball up and down the grassless dirt gridiron. Coach Youngman stands here with his 1928 lightweight team—the year that the school adopted the name Toreadores—who were to form the nucleus of the winning 1929 and 1930 teams. (Courtesy Monterey Public Library, California History Room Archives, the Ann Prego Collection.)

Monterey won the CCAL in 1927 and in 1929. They repeated in 1930 and then went on to beat Burlingame, champion of the Peninsula Athletic League, for the right to play Berkeley in the finals of the North Coast Section of the California Interscholastic Federation. It did not matter that they lost badly to a much larger school in the final game, for this Toreadore squad will be remembered as one of the very good teams in the school's history. There were several standout performers: Keeto Azcarate, John Campbell, Frenchy Cardinale, and Sparky Enea. Perhaps the best of them, and the star of the basketball team as well, was Bricky Crivello. His parents had immigrated from Sicily, and he was born in Monterey and grew up caddying at Pebble Beach. He became the business agent for the Monterey Fisherman's Union for 60 years and was largely responsible for the installation of the bocce ball courts at the Custom House Plaza. (Courtesy Kathryn Alkire.)

"BRICKY"

As abalone attracted Japanese divers to the peninsula coastline, so too came Sicilians to the bay to fish for sardines. Offspring of these immigrants, such as Sparky Enea and Bricky Crivello, began to make their imprint on Monterey High School sports in the late 1920s. Shown here in 1932 is coach Youngman (right), the son of an itinerant preacher, chatting with Dody Russo, whose parents had come to Monterey from Isola delle Femmina near Palermo. (Courtesy Sal Russo.)

The 1938 Toreadore team won the A Division of the CCAL, its first championship since 1930, with a 5-0-2 record against Watsonville, Salinas, Hollister, and Santa Cruz. Mannie Chappel was the leader, while Pete Cardinale, a guard, and Franklin Hayford, an end, were named to the all-conference team. Dooly Bruno, pictured here, was a unanimous All-CCAL selection and gained more yards than any other back in the league. (Courtesy Monterey Public Library, California History Room Archives.)

FOOTBALL

Whenever Monterey High School was out of session, the girls' hockey field became a popular football and baseball venue for younger kids. Of course, the intended use of the field was for girls' athletics, and the photograph at right is of Gloria Wasson, an officer in the Girls Athletic Association, involved in a c. 1950 field hockey game. Just before the war, the always-innovative coach Youngman had put together and directed a clinic for high school instructors and made extensive use of the hockey field. The photograph below shows archery teacher H. C. McQuarrie of Oakland conducting a class there, with the cafeteria on the right and the shop building on the left. Other instructors included Dean Cromwell from the University of Southern California, Everett Dean from Stanford, Tom Stowe from UC Berkeley, and golf professional Peter Hay from Del Monte. (Right, courtesy Gloria Wasson Avila; below, courtesy Sheryl Youngman Mueller.)

The dozen players who logged the most time on coach Youngman's 1942 Toreadore squad were, from left to right, (first row) J. R. Ernest, DeWitt Butler, Don Chick, Don Bergquist, Frank Gida, Ralph Serrano, and Tom Lucido; (second row) Louie Tabayio, Vince Belleci, Joe Colletto, Mike Colletto, and Nick Albert. The two Collettos, uncle Joe and his nephew Mike, were part of a truly outstanding familial sporting tradition. Mike and his brothers Bert and Sal were fine athletes, as was another of Joe's nephews, Jerry, who also played football for Monterey High and was inducted into the Monterey Peninsula College (MPC) Hall of Fame as an integral part of the San Jose State University varsity team. Joe Colletto's own son Jim was a high school All-American at Monterey on a team that went 12-0. He started for the triumphant 1966 UCLA Rose Bowl team and later became the head football coach at Purdue University. But the Colletto dynasty really started with a fighter in the 1930s, Orazio Colletto, known to all as "Tiny." (Courtesy Virginia Albert.)

FOOTBALL

"Tiny" Colletto was 5 feet, 2 inches tall and 1 of 11 children born to parents who immigrated from Isola delle Femmina in Sicily, coming first to Pittsburg in California and then to Monterey. Leaving school after the eighth grade, Colletto joined the navy and while serving aboard the battleship *West Virginia* became flyweight boxing champion of the Pacific Fleet. During the mid-1930s in Monterey, he fought memorable bouts at the recreation center of the Presidio. His ferocity inside the ring and happy-go-lucky lifestyle outside it resulted in an article entitled "Navy Bound" by Carmel writer Tal Josselyn that appeared in *Collier's* magazine and was later made into a movie. In 1940, he and lifetime friend Sparky Enea crewed for John Steinbeck and Ed Ricketts on their voyage to the Sea of Cortez. Boxing had always been well received in Monterey, and this photograph depicts Colletto on the right and Enea on the left as youngsters posing in the ring with Del Monte golf professional Peter Hay. (Courtesy Monterey Public Library, California History Room Archives.)

Many of the school-age young men of Sicilian background in the 1930s and 1940s went out on the family boats when the fish were running and had to adjust their sports activities accordingly. Above is the Colletto's purse seiner, the *U.S. Liberator*, c. 1944. Shown aboard are, from left to right, unidentified, Bert Colletto, Caesar Colletto, Dominick Costanza, unidentified, Nick Giacalone, Jack Aiello, Sal Colletto, Vince Colletto, Dick diPolo, Theodore Canepa, and Tredo Balesteri ("Tiny" Colletto's fight manager and trainer). In the left photograph, brothers Mike (left) and Bert Colletto are shown during a lull in practice on the Monterey High School field. Mike Colletto was a superior athlete, and Bert Colletto was the toughest kid in a tough town. (Above, courtesy Monterey Maritime History Museum, the Captain Sal Colletto Collection; left, courtesy Sal Colletto.)

FOOTBALL

Mike Colletto was an All-CCAL competitor in both football and basketball while he was at Monterey High School. Unfortunately, travel constraints imposed by the wartime economy prevented Colletto and others from showcasing their talents. In 1943, coach Youngman split his squad into two teams in order to create competition. A backfield from that year, from left to right, included (second row) John Light, Joe Anastasia, Colletto, and Wellington Smith. (Courtesy Sal Colletto.)

Sal Colletto was a multisport performer at Monterey High School, and in his senior year of 1947, he shared coach Youngman's outstanding athlete award with Tom Incaviglia. A smart and determined competitor, he was a solid student as well and graduated from Stanford University. The setting for this classic jump-pass was the Monterey High School football field. (Courtesy Sal Colletto.)

Enrollment at Monterey High School dropped during World War II, but by 1946, it was back to full capacity. That year, two fine guards, Roy Forzani and Al Garnero (who was twice all-conference and was named to an All–Northern California team), anchored the line. The following season, the Toreadores won the conference with ease and in non-league play stopped a George Washington team from San Francisco that featured running back Ollie Matson. Joe Grammatico and Bill Krebs were all-conference selections on that 1947 team, as were Bob Baugh and captain Dick Narvaez, both of whom were also listed as honorable mention on at least one All–Northern California team. Pictured here from left to right are team members (first row) unidentified, Forest Millington, Forzani, Krebs, Garnero, Tom Russo, and Vince Aiello; (second row) Secondo Maschio, Sal Colletto, Bob Delgadillo, and Pete Coniglio. (Courtesy Sheryl Youngman Mueller.)

This could have taken place after any football or basketball game of the era—the postgame dance in the gymnasium, heavily chaperoned, with music by a school ensemble. Dancing above, and perhaps the game's heroes, are Sal Colletto with Mary Jane Dietl (left) and Pete Coniglio—later mayor of Monterey—with Lois Magnelli. Colletto would have needed special permission from the school to bring Dietl, a Pacific Grove girl, to a Monterey dance. The photograph at right is of Dietl, the first freshman to win the "golden arrow" for archery excellence at Pacific Grove High. She and Colletto have been married for half a century. (Both courtesy Sal and Mary Jane Colletto.)

For several years, Charlie Frost financed and coached athletics in Monterey. Shown in the above photograph at his football jamboree at the high school in 1943 is his Wildcat team, from left to right: (first row) Horace Battaglia, Richard Lee, Bob Feliciano, Ed Zubov, Ron Roberts, Dick Narvaez, Bob Baugh, Jack Frost, and John Geary; (second row) Felix Spiegler, Jack Holt, Lou Frost, Dan Albert, Don Cummings, Frank Costa, and Vince Maiorana; (third row) Rocky Rundell, C. A. Rundell, Daryl Sanchez, Charlie Frost, and Dan Fowler. Meanwhile, Carmel was beginning to develop its own sports traditions. Their Cobras appear at the jamboree in the photograph below, from left to right: (first row) Perry Brown, Henry Multeni, Treat Arnold, Tom Hefling, Mike Ely, Fred Clarke, and Bob Simmons; (second row) Bill Sapsis, Bob Kolf, Jack Chalkley, and Victor Harbor; (third row) Charlie Frost, unidentified, and ? Kolf.

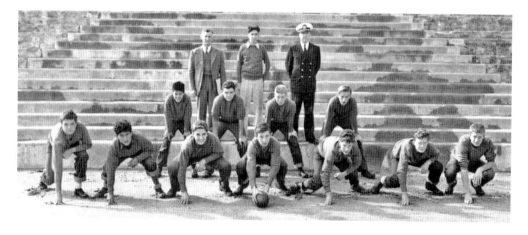

Carmel High School opened for instruction in 1941, the population of the town being just under 3,000 at the time. The 1944 team was a good one, here seen against a backdrop of the beautiful Carmel Valley. Bill Askew, captain for the year, was a standout lineman, and Russ Bohlke a superb running back as well as a fine basketball player. The line consisted of, from left to right, Jim Greenan, Askew, Dennis Gorman, George Moller, Orville Mead, Martin Irwin, Bayard Bardarson; in the backfield were unidentified, Bob Weer, Bohlke, Milt Thompson, and unidentified. At right, leading the cheers for them were, from left to right, Adelle Thompson, Corky Nicholas, and JoAnn Thorn. (Both courtesy Bill Askew Jr.)

Russ Bohlke, of the Carmel High School class of 1944, went up to UC Berkeley with every expectation that he would be able to contribute in a big way to Golden Bear football and basketball programs that were on the verge of national prominence. It was the year that California coach Pappy Waldorf replaced the leather helmet with the new plastic one, and Bohlke, unable to adjust his properly in an early scrimmage, sustained an injury to his cervical vertebrae that left him, in his own words, "A quadriplegic with quite a bit of movement." With inspirational courage, Bohlke has enjoyed a highly involved and productive life. Sometime after the injury, he was asked to serve as honorary cocaptain of a UCLA game, and he is shown here on the California sideline at a "Big Game" with George Souza (left) and Charlie Sarver, who were both out with knee injuries. (Courtesy Russ Bohlke.)

FOOTBALL

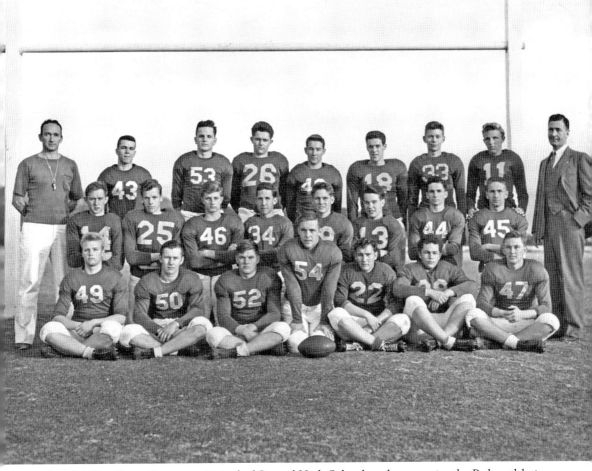

In 1946, Leo Harris became principal of Carmel High School, and to energize the Padre athletic program, he brought in George Mosolf and several other coaches. Harris was rewarded immediately with a league basketball championship in 1946 and a CCAL football winner two years later. Over the many years that he was head coach of everything at Carmel, Mosolf compiled a truly remarkable football record, going undefeated through the late 1940s and the decade of the 1950s. Upon his arrival at the school, he had inherited a bunch of kids who had been together since Miss Riley's first-grade class at Sunset School. Those athletes, from left to right, included (first row) Lew McCreery, Newt Goodrich, Art Harber, Rod Dewar, Dan Holmes, Leslie Bracisco, and Owen Greenan; (second row) Bob Rissell, Elton Clark, Dick Weer, Basil Allaire, Tom Corley, Nelson Byres, Dick Gargiulo, and Paul Warner; (third row) Mosolf, Bob Barry, Floyd Adams, John Blinks, Tom Handley, Bill Hodgson, Mike Monahan, Jim Hare, and coach Donald Craig. (Courtesy Jim Hare.)

Coach Mosolf of Carmel was a stickler for precise positioning, and he used the Chicago Bear playbook. Two of the men on the field through whom he made his system work in 1947 were linemen: captain Rod Dewar (left) and Owen Greenan, who has written fine stories about his youthful experiences on the peninsula. Both Dewar and Greenan were All-CCAL. (Courtesy Owen Greenan.)

Leading the cheers at a c. 1948 Carmel High School game are, from left to right, Dici Douglas, Joan Sanders, Joyce Bannerman, and Georgeanne Bell. Sanders's first cousin was Harry Sanders, an All-CCAL footballer at Monterey High in 1937 and starting halfback at Santa Clara University. She married Gene Vandervort, an all-conference basketball and baseball performer at Carmel, and eight of their grandchildren have played baseball for the Padres. (Courtesy Joan Sanders Vandervort.)

The first of many undefeated football teams under coach George Mosolf at Carmel High was the 1950 squad. They are, from left to right, (first row) Neils Reimers, Mitchell Steinhoudt, Chris Williams, Peter Berg, Bill Daniels, Tom Handley, Sylvester Burger, Bob Updike, and Pierre Boutet; (second row) Mosolf, Don Canham, Henry Overin, Legare McNeill, Jim Hare, Charles Grimshaw, Steve Whitaker, Thor Rasmussen, Dick Weer, Jack Belangee, Frank Cleary, and Charles May. (Courtesy Harrison Memorial Library, Local History Room.)

From the school's inception in 1941, Carmel's natural rival was Pacific Grove, and the symbol of that rivalry came to be a perpetual football trophy known as the "Big Shoe." The original idea came in 1948 from several Carmel players and a Spanish teacher named Miller. The shoe belonged to coach Donald Craig, and J. O. Handley had it bronzed. Jim Hare, an all-conference quarterback who won six letters in his junior year, holds the trophy after the 1949 game. (Courtesy Jim Hare.)

Coach Youngman resigned in 1948 after 20 years at Monterey High School. His team had won the CCAL A Division the year before and was poised for another fine season. The new head football coach was John Gardiner, with his only experience having been a couple of years leading the Toreadore junior varsity as well as the tennis team. He was an easterner with a teaching degree from West Chester State Teachers College in Pennsylvania and had spent World War II as an enlisted man. What he brought to the field was driving ambition and an unlimited sense of life's possibilities. Meeting him for his first practice was a bunch of chip-on-the-shoulder kids from the industrial town on the peninsula. Most of those who would be starters were from immigrant Sicilian or Spanish families, and they were a tough and very talented group. It was a magical season, lasting only a few months; by the following September, most of the boys had graduated and Gardiner had become the head tennis professional at Pebble Beach. (Courtesy Dan Albert.)

FOOTBALL

The 1949 Monterey High School yearbook, *El Susurro*, gushed, "Monterey rooters will long claim 'the Big Green Shirt' of 1948 to be one of the top grid teams ever produced in Northern California and the best ever in the history of the school." It was not a difficult argument to make. The Big Green Shirt rolled over all seven of its opponents—Lowell, Burlingame, San Jose, Watsonville, Hollister, Santa Cruz, and Salinas—scoring 240 points while giving a measly 40. Using John Gardiner's newly installed T-formation, they amassed an average of 356 yards per game. This dominance was achieved with a starting guard, Nat Agliano, weighing in at 145 pounds. The expanded 1948 Toreadore first team consisted of, from left to right, (first row) Nick Marotta, Bill Krebs, Bob Feliciano, Vince Maiorana, Agliano, Pete Torrente, Joe Aquaviva, and Sal Cardinalli; (second row) Joe Grammatico, Al Matthews, Dan Albert, John Anastasia, and Bert Aiello. (Courtesy Sal Cardinalli.)

Seven members of the 1948 Toreadore team were named All-CCAL. Joe Grammatico, pictured here, was being honored so for the second time. The Big Green Shirt was built on character, and all the starters went on to successful lives. Among them, Dan Albert became mayor of Monterey for 20 years, Ronald Reagan appointed Nat Agliano to the Superior Court, and Sal Cardinalli was a standout lineman for San Jose State University. Sal's son Ray later became a first-string linebacker at Stanford. (Courtesy Sal Cardinalli.)

Larry Matthews missed by a year being part of the Big Green Shirt of 1948, but he was one of the finest athletes to ever come through Monterey High School. He was All-CCAL in three sports, and as a multisport performer at San Jose State University, he earned induction into the Spartan Athletic Hall of Fame. Here he is shown picking up yardage for San Jose State against North Texas State University in 1953. (Courtesy Larry and Doris Matthews.)

FOOTBALL

Enormously popular among Monterey fans, Laurence Segovia (right) was a product of Spanish immigrant parentage. His early education was at New Monterey's Bay View School, which turned out top-flight athletes going back to George Parker and Clyde Klaumann in the 1920s and later Tom Perez and the Matthews brothers. Segovia, of the Monterey High class of 1951, was all-conference in football, basketball, and baseball. He was a member of both golf and track teams and was head cheerleader as a freshman. An outstanding all-around athlete at MPC, he was inducted into the Lobo Hall of Fame. While in the U.S. Army at Fort Ord, Segovia (below, right) and Al Matthews (below, left) were members of the 1953 all-star team Gen. Robert McClure assembled that played exhibitions against both the 49ers and the Rams. Segovia topped off his memorable athletic career with five years of professional baseball. (Both courtesy Laurence Segovia.)

Doug McNeil came to Monterey High School in 1946 to coach lightweight sports and eventually became head of the athletic department. His fun-loving side came out among fellow faculty members at events such as the one held by Harlan Watkins at Ed Ricketts's laboratory on Cannery Row, which Watkins had bought from Yak Yee. (Courtesy Sally Schuman.)

These song leaders at Monterey High School appeared in their white corduroy jumpers with the block "M" at games and rallies accompanying the school pep band in 1951–1952. They are, from left to right, (first row) Susan Iino and JoAnn Maiorana; (second row) Pat Mathewson, Polly McKay, Dion Zaches, and Maureen Sinn. (Courtesy Mike Marron.)

FOOTBALL

The Rotary Club award for outstanding back was given to Jack Russo (at right, left) and for outstanding lineman to Doug Forzani (at right, right) for the 1952 football season at Monterey High School. The following year, Forzani was voted the outstanding lineman by his peers at Monterey Peninsula College (MPC). Then known as a junior college, MPC had opened its doors in 1946 as a night school using Monterey High School classrooms and athletic facilities. Within two years, MPC had its own campus and, in 1950, a great football team. The college stayed very close to the peninsula population, and its hall of fame is a virtual who's who of local athletes. Two inductees, Vince Maiorana and Luke Phillips (below), having gone into coaching at the community college level, were voted into the California Community College Football Coaches Hall of Fame. (Right, courtesy Doug Forzani; below, courtesy Luke Phillips.)

Luke Phillips went to Del Monte and Marina Grammar Schools, to Monterey High School, to MPC, and to UC Berkeley. At 5 feet, 5 inches tall, he alternated between the Ramblers and the varsity at Berkeley but made the trip south as a varsity member of the Golden Bears for the Rose Bowl games of 1949 and 1950. He played on General McClure's Fort Ord army teams for a couple of years and then was a student coach with Dick Vermeil and Bill Walsh at San Jose State University under Bob Bronson. In 1963, Phillips was offered the head football coaching position at MPC, a job he held for 23 years. His assistant coaches and great friends were Chris Pappas (left) and Tor Spindler (right), shown here with Phillips (center). After football, he stayed on another 18 years as golf and tennis coach and then retired with advisory responsibilities. (Courtesy Luke Phillips.)

3

BASKETBALL

A Monterey–Pacific Grove rivalry in football, which developed through the 1920s and into the 1930s, was paralleled in basketball. This 1929 Pacific Grove Breaker squad took the measure of the Toreadores in all three categories that were played: midget, lightweight, and varsity, with the latter by a score of 9-6. The following year, the Breakers were again successful, contending with the feared all-around athlete Bricky Crivello by double-teaming him. The Breaker coach during these years, and until he enlisted in the U.S. Navy in 1942, was Charles Easterbrook, seen here at the far right, second row. Charles Gratiot, who was to become a prominent physician on the peninsula, is second from the left in the second row. In the center of the second row is Harry French, a good local tennis player. Bill Davison, second from the right in the first row, was one of the best golfers on the peninsula in the decades after World War II. (Courtesy Pacific Grove High School.)

The term "midget" was used freely through the mid-1930s to denote a special team of the youngest and lightest players or was sometimes used interchangeably with "lightweight." This 1930 midget Breaker team, coached by Charles Easterbrook, included Lefty Davison, the third player from the left, who was to become one of the very good professional baseball players on the peninsula. (Courtesy Pacific Grove High School.)

The 1936–1937 Breaker squad consisted of, from left to right, (first row) Lou Fitzimmons, Darwin Law, Bill Crowley, Davis Perkins, and Paul Cosmey; (second row) Jim Kenyon, John deLorimier, Robert King, and Austen Moore; (third row) coach Easterbrook, Bill Tumbleson, Harry Deffenbaugh, Phil Kenyon, and Kenneth McGill. DeLorimier had three younger brothers, all of whom were starters on the Pacific Grove basketball team. (Courtesy Pacific Grove High School.)

BASKETBALL

While the Depression was dampening athletic enthusiasm at Monterey High School, the Japanese-American Minato Club sports teams thrived. Championship squads were produced, and this is the Lion team that took the regional club title in 1938, anchored by the great Ky Miyamoto. Pictured from left to right are (first row) Jim Tabata, Yoneo Gota, Teruo Esaki, Yo Tabata, and Jim Takigawa; (second row) Oyster Miyamoto, Ky Miyamoto, coach ? Hughes, Kaz Oka, and Archie Miyamoto. (Courtesy Monterey Public Library, California History Room Archives.)

In the Depression year of 1936, Monterey High won the CCAL basketball title and was led by all-conference performers John Burns (second from left, first row) and Harry Sanders (center, first row). Both boys were also members of the best golf team in the school's history, and Sanders became a starting halfback at Santa Clara University under Buck Shaw. A few years later, his fighter was shot down over Germany, and he spent eight months in Stalag 11. (Courtesy Monterey Public Library, California History Room Archives.)

The 1943 Monterey Wildcat hoops squad, seen above, was one Charlie Frost's many kids' athletic teams. They practiced in the "old gym" at the high school, which had been the "new gym" in 1927. Pictured here from left to right are (first row) Vince Basica, Dan Albert, Don Cummings, Mike Marron, Lou Frost, and John Mortenson; (second row) Gene Abinante, Pete Coniglio, Ron Roberts, Bob Baugh, Bill Wardle, Bill Curtis, and Dinky McCormick. The photograph below is of a postgame mingling of Wildcats with the Carmel Destroyers. According to the best Destroyer memory, they won the game 28-23. Pictured from left to right are (first row) Dan Albert, unidentified, Bob Rissell, Murray White, Bob Feliciano, Mike Monahan, Bart DiMaggio, Rod Dewar, Bob Barry, Don Cummings, and Ernie Zanetta; (second row) Richard Lee, Lou Frost, Richard Mulholland, Owen Greenan, Matt Schmutz, Ron Roberts, Lew Mccreery, Frank Costa, Lee Winslow, and Bob Baugh. (Above courtesy author; below courtesy Owen Greenan.)

BASKETBALL

Bay View Elementary School, on Belden Street a few blocks up from the canneries in New Monterey, was a hotbed of fine young athletes during the war years of the 1940s. A number of them later starred at Monterey High School; Laurence Segovia played professional baseball and the Matthews brothers went on to football prominence at San Jose State University. Jeff Jeffries, the school janitor, was the devoted coach of the Bay View Cougars, who are shown here. The members are, from left to right, (first row) Sal Ocampo, Vince Ruiz, unidentified, Segovia, and Lorence Matthews; (second row) unidentified, Roy Perkins, Frank Martin, Tom Arcoleo, unidentified, and Leo Coelho; (third row) chief of police Fred Moore and Jeffries. The photograph below is of a game played at the Bay View auditorium around 1942.

The venue for kids' basketball in Monterey was the lower playground of Walter Colton School at 700 Pacific Street. The first concrete structure had been put up there in 1920 and was called Monterey Grammar School until 1935. In this 1943 photograph, Jack Frost holds the ball, John Douglas is second from the left, and Alfred Avila is at far left.

The 1944–1945 CCAL champion Monterey High School basketball team was one of the best in the school's history. Firmin Gryp led the league in scoring. Shown outside the gymnasium, they are, from left to right, Tony Cusenza, Joe Anastasia, Frank Smith, Eugene Bee, Al Garnero, unidentified, Alex Sanchez, captain Jim Gillette, Bob Weeks, Gryp, Bill Thacker, and Ron Rico. Coach Youngman devised the kneepads worn by Gillette and Rico. (Courtesy Sheryl Youngman Mueller.)

BASKETBALL

This lightweight basketball team at Monterey High School is from 1945–1946 and brought together a collection of outstanding athletes and individuals. Pictured from left to right, they are Dan Albert, Frank Flores, Don Cummings, Al Matthews, and Ray Messinger. Flores was later a member of two national championship track teams at the University of Southern California, cocaptaining in 1952 and competing in the Olympic trials that year. Eventually he joined the faculty of the USC Dental School, where he had done his graduate work. Cummings lettered in varsity basketball and football, was one of many very good swimmers turned out by Monterey High, and later flew jets in the Korean and Vietnam Wars. Matthews was an all-league performer as part of the great 1948 Toreadore football team and played for San Jose State University and for General McClure at Fort Ord. Messinger lettered for three years in varsity basketball, was captain of the tennis team, and graduated from the U.S. Naval Academy. The inspiring success story of the Albert family is chronicled in succeeding photographs. (Courtesy Monterey Public Library, California History Room Archives.)

Emilio Albert migrated to Hawaii from Spain as a contract laborer to pick fruit, but he found his way to Monterey, where he settled in Upper Oak Grove and took employment as a janitor at Monterey High School. His son Nick (left) became a standout athlete at the school during the war years, and Dan (below) lettered all four years in basketball, football, and baseball. Dan was All-CCAL and captain of the basketball team and all-conference and quarterback of the Big Green Shirt football team of 1948. After college, he became head coach of the Toreadore football team for 28 years and mayor of the city for two decades. One of his highlights as mayor was the pride he felt in being able to introduce his mother, who was of humble Spanish origin, to the visiting Juan Carlos, the King of Spain. (Left, courtesy Virginia Albert; below, courtesy Dan Albert.)

BASKETBALL

Nick Albert ran the New Monterey Boys' Club on Hawthorne Street in 1947. His youngest brother, Ed (second from the right, first row) became a running back for the Toreadores. Those pictured are, from left to right, (first row) Joe Favalora, Joe Ciandro, Art Cano, Dominick Canepa, unidentified, Ed Albert, and Joe Rogers; (second row) unidentified, Dick Ciandro, Roland Bispo, John Jone, Vince Ruiz, and Nick Albert. (Courtesy Virginia Albert.)

A great 1949 Pacific Grove team, averaging 6 feet, 2 inches in height, consisting of Dick deLorimier, (No. 6), Max Kelly (No. 5), Joe Sieve, Bill Conlan, and Fred Willson, were nearly stymied by the stalling tactics of Dan Albert (No. 90) and a resourceful Monterey five that was 4-inches-per-man shorter. The half ended 3-2 for the Breakers, who eventually won it and moved on to the Northern California Tournament of Champions.

The Monterey–Pacific Grove sports rivalry in football, dating back to the 1920s, finally ended in 1945 when the two schools stopped scheduling each other, but it continued in basketball. Marty Baskin came to Pacific Grove in 1942 as coach of all sports, but his clear preference was basketball. This action took place in 1952 as Monterey's Jack Frost (left) goes against Tom deLorimier and John Lewis (right).

The construction of Carmel High School was completed in 1941, but its first varsity basketball team played its home games in the Mission Ranch barn. The Padres won their first CCAL basketball championship in 1946, and the team of (pictured from left to right) Lee Laugenour, Jim Hare, Gene Vandervort, Steve Whitaker, and Dick Weer topped the league in 1950. (Courtesy Gene Vandervort.)

BASKETBALL

An outstanding Salinas High five led by Russ Lawler (far left) and Jim Mastin (No. 14) invade the Carmel gymnasium and pick up a win. Visible Padres are Lanny Doolittle (left), Gene Vandervort (No. 22), a deadly outside shot and leading Carmel scorer, and Neils Reimers (No. 25). (Courtesy Gene Vandervort.)

The Carmel High School class of 1950 basketball team stayed together to play for the Carmel Youth Center. The legendary Ky Miyamoto (left, first row), who himself started for the Frost Roofers, acted as player/coach. Next to him is his brother, Gordon Miyamoto, who had pitched brilliantly for the Japanese-American Minato Club in 1949 and was to earn induction into the MPC Hall of Fame. (Courtesy Jim Hare.)

Jim Hare (No. 5), who won six letters as a junior and five as a senior at Carmel High, tries to stop Lorence Matthews, an all-league performer in three sports at Monterey and eventual San Jose State University Hall of Famer. In his professional life, Matthews coached at Los Gatos High School for 37 years and was honored with the dedication of a field house in his name. (Courtesy Lorence Matthews.)

Nick Giovinazzo in his first year coached the 1952 Monterey lightweights. Pictured here are members of the team, from left to right: (first row) Troy Petty, John Souza, Ron Linares, Barney Belleci, and Dick Kobayashi; (second row) Vince Torrente, George Yamanishi, Anthony Russo, Ray Cardinale, Dominick Mineo, and Don Davison; (third row) manager Lyman Wermuth, Joe Indorato, Frank Casas, Giovinazzo, Jim Stewart, Albert McKinney, and Karl Ohrt. Cardinale and Mineo were All-CCAL. (Courtesy Ray Cardinale.)

BASKETBALL

"The greatest M.U.H.S. basketball team ever," enthused the Monterey High yearbook about their basketball team. The 1952 CCAL A Division champion Toreadores went 19-5, including a sweep of the Carmel Tournament. It was the first-ever trip for Monterey to the Tournament of Champions at Berkeley, and it resulted in the conquest of the consolation event after an overtime loss to San Francisco City champion George Washington. Jack Frost (above, left) and Don Minick (above, right) were unanimous All-CCAL selections, and both were *San Francisco Examiner* honorable mention All–Northern California. The photograph at right portrays the team's locker room after a win: jubilation centers on Vince Tomasello (seated).

Monterey High School basketball coach Ed Larsh is in the back of the photograph, next to county supervisor Sam Karas (No. 85). The party was on Cannery Row in the wooden building with the stairs up the front that had been inhabited for many years by Ed Ricketts, the researcher made famous through John Steinbeck's *Cannery Row* and *Sea of Cortez*. Host Harlan Watkins, in front of Karas and Larsh, bought the place in 1949 from Yak Yee when he, Watkins, began teaching. At the school, Watkins organized a rooters' club of sports enthusiasts that numbered in the hundreds who were committed to attending all games, both home and away. He also offered a memorable senior class for handpicked students in World Literature, often utilizing Ed Ricketts's laboratory for evening sessions. Also shown at this gathering is tennis coach Dick Schuman (No. 89). (Courtesy Sally Schuman.)

4

TENNIS

Guests began playing tennis on the Monterey Peninsula when the fabulous Hotel Del Monte was built in the 1880s, but it took until the 1920s for a cadre of local players to develop. Even then, much of the peninsula's tennis continued to take place on courts that were within the purview of the Del Monte Properties and its gated real estate. One such venue, Cheviot Hills, was the residence of Col. and Mrs. Allen Griffin that was set on 20 acres near Cypress Point. There were stables, imported flowers in the gardens, and the finest tennis court on the peninsula. From left to right are Colonel Griffin, owner of the *Monterey Herald*; Ro Arlen, daughter of actor Richard Arlen; Hester Hately Griffin, great-aunt of actress Glenn Close; and local resident Charlie Frost, who, along with Walter Snook and Bill Dekker, played at Cheviot Hills almost daily when Charlie Chaplin spent a couple of summers at Pebble Beach in the mid-1930s. Tennis would be followed by tea and lively conversation.

From its inception in 1882 to its closure 60 years later, the Hotel Del Monte attracted great players to its tennis events. Bill Johnston, Helen Wills, Don Budge, Bobby Riggs, and Alice Marble performed there. It has been suggested that the idea for the Davis Cup matches was born at the hotel when Dwight Davis played in the first East-West team matches on its courts in 1899.

The Monterey Peninsula Country Club opened its doors in July 1926 and encouraged local membership. It had put in two tennis courts and ran events to promote its usage. Mary Callender, daughter of the golf professional at the club, won the mixed doubles at this tournament in 1929. Her partner was Pacific Grove High School player Harry French.

In the mid-1920s, the owner of the Forest Hill Hotel in Pacific Grove donated a block of property with a tennis court on it to the city, and four more courts were added later. The high school team played their matches there. This is the 1931 squad. Dick Schuman, the little fellow on the far right in the first row, led the Breaker netmen to the North Coast Section Tournament in 1933. (Courtesy Pacific Grove High School.)

John Campbell, of the class of 1932 and a four-year letterman in football and baseball, played No. 1 singles for the Monterey High tennis team in his senior year. In the 1950s and 1960s, he coached tennis and taught history at the school. Here he is shown (left) in these later years with an old Pacific Grove nemesis, Dick Schuman. (Courtesy Sally Schuman.)

Monterey High School constructed eight courts in 1932 and by the early years of the war, led first by Spencer Kern and then by Don Chick, had begun to assert tennis dominance in the CCAL. Pictured here are Bill Wardle (left) and Everett Messinger, the boys who won the North Coast Section Doubles Tournament held at Stanford in 1946. (Courtesy Everett Messinger.)

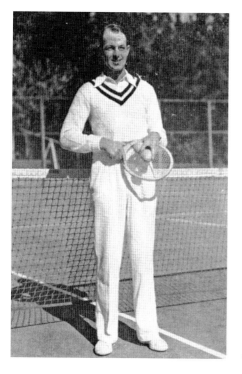

Tennis professional Leo Kohler came to the Hotel Del Monte before World War II and went over to Pebble Beach with its three courts and wooden shack after it was over. In April 1947, he staged the first annual Northern California Interscholastic Tournament there.

An excellent teacher and true lover of the game of tennis, Leo Kohler quickly developed a following at Pebble Beach of avid young players. Here several of them gather at his house in Carmel for the annual Northern California Interscholastic Tournament draw on the eve of the event in 1947. Pictured from left to right are George Langan, Pat Timbers, Jack Frost, Jennifer Lloyd, and Lou Frost.

John Gardiner came to Monterey in 1946 as a teacher and football coach and moved in with the Frost family. Within a short time, he became involved with tennis, and here he is seen (center) at the trophy table of a county tournament in 1947 at Monterey High School. With him are, from left to right, Anne Fratessa, Barbara Bebb, Jack Frost, and Lee Winslow.

The Monterey High tennis courts by Herrman Drive are the scene of this assemblage of John Gardiner tennis acolytes. They are, from left to right, (first row) Peter Krogh, unidentified, Ray March, Henry Fisher, and Warren Masten; (second row) John Mortenson, Dick Brownlee, John Douglas, Mike Marron, Franklin Young, and Gardiner. (Courtesy Mike Marron.)

The second annual Northern California Interscholastic Tournament, held at Pebble Beach the year before, moved over to Monterey in 1948. In overwhelming response, more than 250 youngsters converged on the area and were housed and fed privately and at Asilomar. The cover of the tournament program featured the classic backhand of Monterey's Ray Messinger.

The quantity and quality of the participation in the Northern California Interscholastic Tournament prompted an article in the July issue of *American Lawn Tennis* asserting that Monterey was "rapidly becoming recognized as the junior tennis capital of Northern California." Pictured is a final being played between Monterey favorite Jack Frost and Berkeley's Clif Mayne in the 15-and-under division. (Courtesy Mike Marron.)

Monterey High School principal and enthusiastic tennis player Thor Krogh presents a winner's trophy to Jack Frost at the 1948 Northern California Interscholastic Tournament. John Gardiner is at the microphone. In the background are, from left to right, Miriam Rumwell, Claire Vedensky, Nancy Ewer, and Lorraine Steinfeld.

In 1948, Leo Kohler moved from Pebble Beach to Salt Lake City and within a decade was back to stay in Monterey. He brought with him a wife, the former Marjorie Rowe, who was to become one of the best senior players in the world and represented the United States at the Marble Cup in Perth.

When Leo Kohler left Pebble Beach in 1948, John Gardiner resigned from Monterey High School and took the tennis position that Kohler had vacated. A year earlier, Gardiner married the former Barbara Jane Seymour of Eldorado, Kansas. She was given in marriage by Charlie Frost, on her left, and Lee Weston (left) was her attendant. Bill Hawthorne (right) , a member of the Monterey High School faculty, was the best man.

TENNIS

DEL MONTE PROPERTIES COMPANY

Del Monte, California

September 9, 1949

S. F. B. MORSE
Chairman of the Board

Dear Charlie:

I have watched the career of your son
with great interest, particularly as
we used to play so much tennis together,
I haven't seen him perform as yet.
Does he get around the courts the way
you used to?   You could cover more
territory than anyone I ever saw. Now
that young Jack is making The Beach Club
his home club his career becomes particularly interesting to us.

Kindest personal regards.

Sincerely,

Sam Morse

Mr. Charles L. Frost
Box 871
Monterey, California

S. F. B. Morse, an Andover and Yale man and distant relative of the inventor of the telegraph, came out to San Francisco in 1907 and eventually was employed by the Crocker interests to liquidate their Pacific Improvement Company. In a stroke of genius, he organized financial backing and bought the Monterey Peninsula properties for himself under the aegis of the Del Monte Properties Company, through which he developed a tourist paradise with world-class golf courses and other recreational facilities. Morse had been captain of his Yale football team and always loved sports. He noted the progress being made by a young tennis player over the hill in Monterey and, in a spirit of thoughtfulness, sent a Beach Club membership to the 15-year-old. The letter is to Charlie Frost, the boy's father, who had been a friend of Morse in the early days.

Dick Schuman was a very good high school player at Pacific Grove and further honed his game at St. Mary's College in the middle of the Depression. He came to teach at Monterey High School after World War II, and when John Gardiner left for Pebble Beach in 1949, he took over as tennis coach. He was a big man and a fine player with a ferocious western forehand. (Courtesy Mike Marron.)

Popular with students, tennis coach Dick Schuman (left) also got along well with fellow faculty members. Here he is joined by teacher Harlan Watkins (center), basketball coach Ed Larsh (right), and county supervisor Sam Karas (kneeling), who appear to be rushing to the aid of Carol Todd. The party was on Cannery Row at Ed Ricketts's laboratory, which was owned and inhabited by Watkins. (Courtesy Sally Schuman.)

In the 1948–1949 interclub season, the Monterey Peninsula entrant won the Northern California title by beating San Jose in the finals. The following year, it lost 5-4 to Palo Alto in the last match. All-Navy champion Elston Wyatt was a strong No. 1 for Monterey, while Dick Schuman and 14-year-old Jack Frost alternated at Nos. 2 and 3. Wyatt and Schuman were a very good doubles team. Pictured in the above photograph from left to right are unidentified, Schuman, Wyatt, Frost, Dick Williams, and unidentified. The photograph below shows Schuman (left) and Wyatt (second from left) following a three-set loss to former Stanford players Fred and Bob Lewis. (Both courtesy Sally Schuman.)

Jack Frost of Monterey won the national 15-and-under title on the clay courts at Kalamazoo, Michigan, in August 1949. He is shown on center court immediately after the final against Al Kuhn of Evanston, Illinois. Ball boy Brooks Godfrey (left) and fellow player Stan Canter offer congratulations.

Dick Schuman became tennis coach at Monterey High School in 1949 and kept the team atop the CCAL conference, a position the Toreadores had held since before the war. The 1950 squad included, from left to right, (first row) Jim Lewis, Randy Reinstedt, John Logan, Lawrence Chan, and John Douglas; (second row) Schuman, John Mortenson, Chris Wojciechowski, Bob Woodward, Mike Marron, John McCrary, and Jack Frost.

TENNIS

Bob Clark (right) came to Monterey High School in 1949 as an assistant basketball coach, having himself starred at Pepperdine University. The following year, he helped Dick Schuman with the tennis team and eventually became athletic director. He is engaging here in a time-honored tennis activity—squeegeeing the courts after a rain. Working with him are Mike Marron (center) and John Mortenson. (Courtesy Mike Marron.)

The Monterey High School yearbook announced to the world that the 1951 tennis team was "probably the best team in California and one of the best in the United States." Indeed, the Toreadore netters took on the best in the state—Santa Monica, South Pasadena, University High, and Ventura—and held its own. The 1951 team shown in the photograph includes, from left to right, coach Schuman, John Mortenson, Mike Marron, John Logan, Randy Reinstedt, Anthony Russo, Jack Frost, and coach Clark. (Courtesy Mike Marron.)

The annual Northern California Interscholastic Tournaments in Monterey gave a multitalented local girl the chance to showcase her ability. Pat Hoang was born on Cannery Row into a Chinese American family, learned tennis on the high school courts, and by the time she was 12 was ranked third in Northern California in her age division. Two years later, she won the 15-and-under event at the tournament. At school, she used her art-class project to design the family house in New Monterey, and she was class valedictorian. She had given up tennis by the time she enrolled at UC Berkeley, where she graduated Phi Beta Kappa. This photograph was taken after a doubles final at the Northern California Interscholastic Tournament in 1950. Standing from left to right are Betty Mitchell, Hoang, Luzon Hanson, and Beverly Mater. (Courtesy Mike Marron.)

Gertrude Beall was the finest female tennis player produced on the Monterey Peninsula over the first half of the 20th century. She was smart, could run and hit with pace, and was good under fire. She won the 18-and-under Northern California Interscholastic Tournament in Monterey in 1951 and the national hardcourt doubles later in the year. In 1952, she won the California State Junior Women's Tournament and was ranked ninth in the United States. After high school, she went to Monterey Peninsula College, where she competed as the only woman on the men's team. Her record there earned her Hall of Fame recognition. Beall was awarded her bachelor of arts degree from UC Berkeley. Here she is, at center, scooping up balls at Pebble Beach around 1950 with, from left to right, Tim Gallwey (who was to author *The Inner Game of Tennis*), Annette Stoesser, Jean Fratessa, and George Stoesser.

After attending college, Gertrude Beall Woods (left), now with a family and living in Alameda, limited her play to Bay Area events. In 1963, she faced Helen Wong in a final in Livermore. Wong had been a very good junior tennis and basketball player in San Francisco in the late 1940s. (Courtesy Gertrude Beall Woods).

When John Gardiner (left) went over to Pebble Beach, he engaged the services of Don Prince (second from the left). Prince starred in tennis, basketball, and football at MPC, was inducted into the school's Hall of Fame, and earned his bachelor of arts from UC Berkeley in optometry. Ready for instruction (to the right of Prince) are, from left to right, Tom Gardiner, unidentified, Bill Stahl, Lawson Little, Patricia Farish, Cameron Butts, and Pam Hately. (Courtesy Don Prince.)

TENNIS

Jack Frost was the first player ever selected from the Monterey Peninsula to compete in the national tournament for boys and juniors at Kalamazoo, Michigan. In his first year, 1948, he was in the semifinals of the 15-and-under, and the following year he won it. Three years later, he captured the 18-and-under crown, the first Northern Californian to do so since Don Budge in 1933. At right is a photograph of Frost moments after the finals. His success at Kalamazoo was followed by an appointment to the U.S. Davis Cup team for its match against Canada. Frost is at the far left, third row, in the photograph below, taken at the match. The other players representing the United States were Vic Seixas (fourth from left, second row), Herb Flam (third from left, third row), and Bob Perry (second from left, third row).

An exhibition match is in progress in 1954 at Pebble Beach between Jack Frost of Monterey and Stanford University and Tom Brown, a 1946 Wimbledon finalist. John Gardiner, who had been football and tennis coach at Monterey High School, was now the head tennis professional at the Beach Club.

Stanford University inducted Jack Frost into its athletic Hall of Fame. In 1956, he was a finalist in the NCAA Tournament, losing on the clay at Kalamazoo, Michigan, to USC import Alex Olmedo of Peru. Following his military service, Frost competed in six Wimbledons, earned a doctorate in history, with Arabic and Swahili as examining languages, was in the Sudan on a Fulbright Research Grant, and lived for some years in Vienna.

5

GOLF

The Monterey Peninsula produced legendary athletic teams and individuals over the first half of the 20th century, but it was also home to at least two legendary sporting venues. One was the Pebble Beach Golf Links, with its spectacular views over the Pacific Ocean. Its grand opening was in 1919, along with the nearby and newly built lodge. The Pebble Beach Links was one of three courses built by Sam Morse in the Del Monte Forest out of property that he, as liquidator for the Pacific Investment Corporation, shrewdly held out for himself and made the centerpiece of his Del Monte Properties Company. The photograph here is of a breathtaking view from the lodge over the terrace, the 18th green, and the waters of the Pacific. (Courtesy Monterey Public Library, California History Room Archives.)

The principal designer and architect of the Pebble Beach Golf Links, which opened for play in 1919, was Jack Neville. He crafted the course so well that barely any changes had to be made to meet modern standards 53 years later when Pebble Beach hosted the U.S. Open. A fine golfer himself, Neville won the California amateur championship five times, twice at the Pebble Beach Links he had designed. In 1923, he was named to the U.S. Walker Cup team to compete against Great Britain at St. Andrew's. Standing with Neville (left) in the photograph below is the great Bobby Jones. (Both courtesy Monterey Public Library, California History Room Archives.)

In less than 10 years after his acquisition of Del Monte Forest, Sam Morse developed what would endure as two legendary golf courses. The Pebble Beach Golf Links was one, and Cypress Point was the other. The architect of the latter was Scotsman Dr. Alister MacKenzie, but the inspiration for Cypress Point and some of the actual design came from Marion Hollins, the 1921 U.S. Women's Amateur champion. MacKenzie worked closely with Hollins on the entire layout of the course and publicly credited her with designing the 230-yard 16th, arguably the most famous hole in golfdom. The course was completed in 1928, and Hollins served on the first board of directors of the club. (Courtesy Monterey Public Library, California History Room Archives; photograph by Ansel Adams.)

Marion Hollins won the U.S. Women's Amateur Golf Championship in 1921, the Pebble Beach Women's Championship in 1923 and for years thereafter, and captained the U.S. Curtis Cup team in 1932. Hollins was also an expert rider, an avid polo player, and one of the first women to drive a race car. Born to wealth on Long Island, she made her own fortune investing in California oil exploration, and, working with Sam Morse and the Del Monte Properties Company, she bought heavily into Monterey County real estate. At one time, Hollins owned the 2,000 acres that later became the Carmel Valley Village and the Holman Ranch. She also conceived of and directed the construction of Cypress Point Golf Course. She is shown teeing off at the Monterey Peninsula Country Club in the late 1920s. (Courtesy Monterey Public Library, California Reading Room Archives.)

The setting is the clubhouse at the nine-hole Pacific Grove Municipal Golf Course, which opened in 1934 on land donated to the city by Sam Morse. The two gentlemen are unrelated, and neither played golf, but both fathered golfing dynasties and both were witnesses at the process leading to canonization of Fr. Junipero Serra, founder of the Carmel Mission. On the right is Mark Fry, who fathered five sons—all of them golf professionals. One of these was Fred X. Fry, the longtime professional at the Pacific Grove course, who himself fathered a golfing family. Son Larry Fry competed in the National Junior Championship in 1952, and his older brother Gerry, who was also an outstanding golfer, became mayor of Monterey. On the left is Abel N. Espinosa, who fathered 10 children, 6 of whom became golf professionals. Two of the sons gained international prominence as touring players, and a daughter, Annette, became the first woman golf teacher in California. (Courtesy Felix Spiegler.)

The Abel Espinosa family of Monterey produced six professional golfers. Annette (left, driving at Pebble Beach) was the first woman teaching professional in California and lived to be 106 years old. Her five golfing brothers learned the game while caddying at Del Monte when they were kids. Through the late 1920s and early 1930s, Al Espinosa won nine events on the PGA tour and lost in the finals of the PGA Championship in 1928 and then to Bobby Jones in a playoff at the U.S. Open in 1929. He was on three Ryder Cup teams. Brother Abe Espinosa (below, second from left), who is seen here with Bobby Jones (far right), won the Western Open at North Shore in 1928 and the Texas Open in San Antonio in 1931. (Both courtesy Felix Spiegler.)

Cam Puget is in the center of this photograph with the great Lawson Little (second from right). It was taken at the Monterey Peninsula Country Club, where Puget had become head professional in 1937 and was to stay for 24 years. Meanwhile, his brother Henry landed the head job at Cypress Point. The Puget family moved to the peninsula in 1917 and settled in Oak Grove close to the golf clubhouse at Del Monte. The kids caddied there and sneaked onto the course to practice golf. The Espinosa brothers learned to play well enough doing this that two of them became top-level touring players. Another young caddy, Olin Dutra, went on to win 19 tour events in the depths of the Depression, including the PGA match-play championship in 1932 and the U.S. Open two years later at Merion. Topping off his brilliant career, Dutra played in the 1933 and 1935 Ryder Cup matches. (Courtesy W. Lawson Little.)

The Monterey Peninsula Country Club in the Del Monte Forest was an important piece in Sam Morse's vision of a vast recreational empire. The Dunes Course, engineered by Seth Raynor, and the clubhouse were opened in 1926 along with two tennis courts, a swimming hole, and a bathhouse by Point Joe. Member Barney Segal (right) is shown on the Dunes Course in 1929.

Monterey High School added golf as a sport in 1928 and between 1935 and 1939 fielded among the best teams in the country. The heart of these Toreadore squads was comprised of four young men who learned their golf through junior memberships at the Monterey Peninsula Country Club. Three of them are seen here: John Burns and Warner Keeley are second and third from the left and Bud Brownell is fifth from the left. (Courtesy Sheryl Youngman Mueller.)

This was the best golf team in the history of Monterey High School. Standing on the football field, they are, from left to right, Harry Sanders, Harvey Breaux, Warner Keeley, Bud Brownell, John Burns, and coach Hal Youngman. Breaux and Keeley, both of whom would have been No. 1 anywhere else, fought it out for the No. 2 slot behind Brownell. Sanders and Burns were tough competitors, both earning all-conference honors in basketball and Sanders in football as well. Brownell remains a local legend and might have gone on to become one of the greats. He won the Northern California Juniors in 1939, was Stanford University champion in 1941, and was runner-up in the National Intercollegiate Tournament. In 1943, he was commissioned into the service, and as an attack transport crewmember, he was at most of the Pacific landings and was cited for bravery under fire. Brownell was at the Leyte and Luzon invasion, and just after that he was killed in action in the Philippines. (Courtesy Sheryl Youngman Mueller.)

Over the years, Monterey High golf teams conducted their practices at the Hotel Del Monte course, which opened in 1897 and today is the oldest golfing venue in continuous use west of the Mississippi. Del Monte hosted the Pacific Coast Open in 1901, and the Pacific Coast Golf Association's amateur championships soon followed, as did Del Monte's own highly prestigious tournament. (Courtesy Monterey Public Library, California History Room Archives.)

Immediately following World War II, Felix Spiegler (left) was the top golfer at Monterey High School and one of the best in the conference. The son of Annette Espinosa Spiegler, he is shown here playing a round with his uncle Abe in 1960. Spiegler became a navy flier and retired as a captain, having flown in the Korean and Vietnam Wars. (Courtesy Felix Spiegler.)

During and after World War II, Monterey High School had consistently good teams, one truly outstanding junior player in Peter Geyer, and an eccentric coach. The coach was history teacher Wayne Edwards, who had come to the school in 1927 and whose practice it was to employ his chow dog, Mr. Wong, to caddy for him. The 1950 team, from left to right, included Edward Cortes, Vince Tomasello, Geyer, Joe Kirby, Ernie Cortes, and Edwards.

One of the best junior players in the country at the start of the 1950s, Peter Geyer twice won the Call-Bulletin Tournament in San Francisco, won the Jaycee in Long Beach, and was runner-up in the Northern California Juniors. He competed twice in the nationals, reaching the semifinals in 1952. Here he is chatting with that year's national junior champion, Tommy Jacobs, who went on to a fine professional career. (Courtesy Gretchen Geyer Bartowick.)

Buck Henneken and Mary Sargent were the dominant golfers on the Monterey Peninsula during the 1940s and 1950s. Henneken was Monterey Peninsula Country Club champion five times and played in the U.S. Amateur Championship. Here he is shown, with the hat, on the 18th hole at Del Monte. His opponent is Bill Davison, another superb golfer. (Courtesy Don Davison.)

Scotsman Peter Hay was head professional at Pebble Beach from 1942 to 1961, and while he was there, he designed the nine-hole Peter Hay Course next to the Lodge. Here he is shown with a group of Monterey area juniors at a tournament at Pebble Beach in 1950. They are, from left to right, (first row) unidentified, Adrian Montiel, Hay, winner Peter Geyer, and Andy Gonzalez; (second row) Vince Ruiz, two unidentified, and Edward Cortes. (Courtesy Monterey Public Library, California History Room Archives.)

It has been said of longtime Pebble Beach resident Lawson Little that he was the greatest match player in the history of golf. In 1934, he won his Walker Cup match and the same year captured both the British and U.S. Amateur titles. The next year he did it again. As a professional, he won the Canadian, the Los Angeles, and the U.S. Open tournaments. He was given the Sullivan Award as the nation's outstanding amateur athlete and was later inducted into the PGA's Hall of Fame. Evidenced in the photograph above is his tremendous power. Below, he is seen (left) at Pebble Beach in discussion with Peter Hay (back), Ben Hogan (center), and actor Glen Ford during the filming of *Follow the Sun*, the story of Hogan's life as a golfer. (Both courtesy W. Lawson Little.)

Pictured from left to right are Lawson Little, Francis Brown, Ed Lowery, and World Golf Hall of Famer Byron Nelson about to tee off at Cypress Point during the 1950 Crosby Tournament. Twenty years earlier, Brown had held the amateur titles of Japan, California, and Hawaii concurrently. He owned a house at Pebble Beach and died there, but his ancestral home was on the island of Hawaii where he grew up and spent most of his time. There he lived among the fishponds of the Kohala Coast with his lady friend, Winona Love, and eventually developed the property into the Mauna Lani resort. One of his grandfathers was a native Hawaiian of exalted rank, and Brown himself was a territorial representative and then a U.S. senator. (Courtesy W. Lawson Little.)

Popular singer and matinee idol Bing Crosby is seen following through while on a war-bond tour. When peace returned, Crosby brought world-class golf to the Monterey Peninsula with his first annual pro-am tournament in 1947. In the early years, the format called for play at Cypress Point on Friday, the Dunes Course at Monterey Peninsula Country Club on Saturday, and Pebble Beach on Sunday. (Courtesy W. Lawson Little.)

Ted Durein (right) joined the *Herald* newspaper in Monterey in 1935 and was there as reporter, sports editor, and managing editor for 40 years. Although not a golfer himself, he was responsible for bringing to Bing Crosby's attention the merit of moving the crooner's 18-hole tournament from Rancho Santa Fe to the Monterey Peninsula and making it a 54-hole event. (Courtesy Monterey Public Library, California History Room Archives.)

A mid-1950s publicity shot brought together some of the local citizenry most involved in staging the early Crosby Tournaments. Perched atop the contraption from left to right are Roland Ingles, Ted Durein (on rear perch), Gwenn Graham, Bud Giles, Alvan Privette, Peter Hay, Chester Gillette, Hank Ketcham, Julian Graham, Tinsley Fry, and Dan Searle. Julian Graham was the independent official photographer for Del Monte Properties from 1924 to 1963 with time taken out to cover the first Japanese bombing raids over China in the mid-1930s. His wife, Gwenn Graham, also worked for Del Monte, creating and running the Councours d'Elegance automobile show for its first 18 years. Hank Ketcham was creator and writer of the "Dennis the Menace" cartoon strip. (Courtesy W. Lawson Little.)

6

SWIMMING

In 1894, Lou Hare became the first elected Monterey County surveyor. His home was in Salinas, but he kept rooms at the Casa Sanchez on Alvarado Street in Monterey. He often brought his daughter Dorothy over from Salinas and encouraged her to develop her swimming skills in the bay or at the Hotel Del Monte plunge. In this photograph, Hare (lower left) with hat and lighting a cigar, is at the Pacific Grove beach in 1914. His teenage daughter wears a heavy coat and, with the band as a backdrop, looks back at the camera.

The Pacific Grove beach, with its cement pier at the foot of Forest Avenue, was a safe place for swimmers and a popular gathering spot. Various kinds of boats were available for rent; Dorothy Hare and her cousin are shown in a rowboat on the bay in 1914.

For secure swimmers, aquaplaning was offered from the Pacific Grove pier. Sharks, including great whites, lurked out in the bay. Nonetheless, county supervisor Lou Hare often took his young daughter far out from shore to aquaplane or simply to swim back.

SWIMMING

By 1915, the three peninsula towns of Monterey, Carmel, and Pacific Grove together had a population of around 8,000 to enjoy the coastal waters and sands. In the summer months, the number was augmented by enthusiasts from Salinas and other inland towns and ranches. The Hotel Del Monte had a bathhouse and access to the inviting beach that extended over to the wharf in Monterey. Pictured here are four Salinas High School girls seated on a beached rowboat at Del Monte around 1916. They are, from left to right, Doris Anderson, Irene Hughes, Dorothy Hare, and Lois Anderson. Below, the four girls test the water.

The sumptuous Hotel Del Monte with its Roman plunge filled with warmed seawater is the setting for this 1917 image. Diving is Dorothy Hare, who learned to swim here, in the bay, and in the Carmel River. She swam on the team at Stanford University and fully 75 years after her graduation, when the rush was on to recognize women in sports, the university awarded her a block "S."

Tassajara Hot Springs is buried deep in the Ventana Wilderness south of Monterey and was known to Native American tribes throughout the area for hundreds of years. In 1890, Chinese laborers blasted a hair-raising, one-way, horse-and-buggy road from solid rock. Dorothy Hare, at the far right, and her friends went in on horseback to relish the hot, curative waters of the pool. The year was 1914.

It is summer 1917 at Cachagua on the upper reaches of the Carmel River. In April, President Wilson had asked Congress for a formal declaration of war against Germany, and a vicious strain of influenza was beginning to work its way through the land. The girls had just graduated from high school and were enjoying lazy summer days. They are, from left to right, Dorothy Winkle, Dorothy Hare, Doris Anderson, and Lois Anderson.

Two pals are honing their swimming skills at the mouth of the Carmel River and enjoying the blazing white-sand beach there. The river courses down the length of the Carmel Valley and washes over a sandbar into the Pacific Ocean. The year is 1943, and the country is at war.

Through the prosperous 1920s, the population of the peninsula towns put together nearly doubled from 9,000 to 17,000. Yet for the part of the public that did not have access to the pool at the Hotel Del Monte or the Monterey Peninsula Country Club, the available venues for swimming continued to be the beaches and rivers. Here a group of Pacific Grove High School swimmers pose above the beach at the foot of Forest Avenue. (Courtesy Pacific Grove High School.)

Ironically, despite economic depression and stagnant population growth on the peninsula, the 1930s saw the construction of several major sports venues: the municipal baseball park and golf course in Pacific Grove and eight tennis courts at Monterey High School. For swimmers, the City of Pacific Grove saltwater plunge, pictured here, was dedicated in 1935 as well as the Monterey High School pool.

SWIMMING

In 1936, Monterey High had a new swimming pool and its first organized team—one of the few schools in the region to recognize the sport. Following World War II, Monterey scored well at the North Coast Section meets. The coach of note was Frank Young, pictured here, who was highly respected by his swimmers. Future great Pete Cutino wrote in later years of his early mentor, "Coach Young knew how to condition us and get us ready to compete; we had faith in him." Apart from Cutino, there were many other fine swimmers at the school who thrived under Young's tutelage: Don Cummings, Ben Dew, Bob Pietrobono, the Googins brothers (Tom, Bill, and Jerry), Hitoshi Kono, and backstroker Ken Kimball, who went on to earn All-American honors at Monterey Peninsula College.

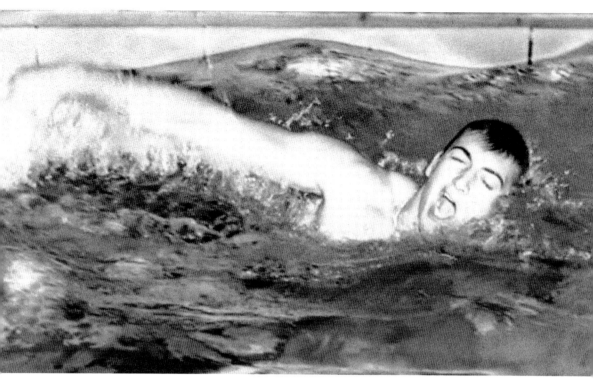

In the postwar era, Monterey High School produced a legend in Pete Cutino. His people were Sicilians from Isola delle Femmina, near Palermo, who had come to Monterey to fish for sardines, and young Cutino toughened his mind and body working on the family purse seiner. As many local kids had done before, Cutino learned to swim among the pilings of the wharf and in the bay, and, with those of his generation, by sneaking into the high school pool at night. He received his early formal education from the Franciscans at San Carlos School and then entered Monterey High preceded by a reputation as a competitor and a gifted swimmer. Under coach Frank Young's regimen, he fulfilled his promise, became an outstanding freestyle swimmer, and was prepared for the challenges of the higher levels that were to come. (Courtesy Louise Cutino.)

After a year at MPC, Pete Cutino received his bachelor and master of arts degrees from California Polytechnic State University, San Luis Obispo, where he competed in swimming and water polo. He finished with multiple school swimming records and was selected three times to the all-conference water polo team. Eventually he was inducted into Halls of Fame at both schools. Above, Cutino is shown on the pool deck, preparing to launch into his specialty, the 200-yard freestyle; below, he sits on a diving board in San Luis Obispo at 22 years of age in 1955. (Both courtesy Louise Cutino.)

The University of California
Intercollegiate Athletic Department
in association with the Big C Society

cordially invites you to the ninth annual

CALIFORNIA HALL OF FAME
INDUCTION BANQUET

on Friday, October 28, 1994
at the Berkeley Marina Marriott Hotel

6:00 p.m. No-host cocktails
7:00 p.m. Dinner

Kindly respond by October 14, 1994

1994 Inductees

Pete Cutino	Head Coach - Water Polo
Larry Friend	Basketball
Miles "Doc" Hudson	Head Coach - Rugby
Paul Larson	Football
Sylvie Monnet	Volleyball
Irvine Phillips	Football, Track & Field
Ron Rivera	Football
Graham Smith	Swimming
Gerald Stratford	Tennis
Jack Yerman	Track & Field, Football

In 1963, Pete Cutino became coach of water polo and swimming at UC Berkeley, and in his 26 years there, he won 8 NCAA titles and 13 national championships. By the end of his coaching career, Cutino had served as head of both the U.S. National and the Olympic water polo teams. He was inducted into the UC Berkeley (left) and the U.S. Water Polo Halls of Fame, and the San Francisco Olympic Club established the Peter J. Cutino Award to be presented annually to the top male and female water polo players in the United States. In his retirement, he wrote a delightful book about his formative years on the peninsula entitled *Monterey; a View from Garlic Hill*. Below, Cutino (left) shares a chat with actor Jack Palance. (Courtesy Louise Cutino.)

7

RIDING

Tom Dorrance (right) was born in 1910, and his life spanned most of the 20th century. He spent the better part of that time learning from horses and passing along to humans what he had discovered. At the Dorrance Ranches in the Sierra de Salinas, he revolutionized the training of horses long before the film industry brought the idea of "horse whispering" to public attention. Dorrance shunned personal celebrity, but toward the end of his life, his peers accorded him the highest recognition. He was recipient of the Chester Reynolds Award from the National Cowboy Hall of Fame, the Vaquero Award from the National Reined Cow Horse Association, and the Lavin Cup from the American Association of Equine Practitioners. Here he instructs Roy Forzani, whose own roots go deep into the Carmel Valley and who himself had a vast knowledge of horsemanship. (Courtesy Doug Forzani.)

Cowboy Roy Forzani's maternal grandmother, Maria Tomasa Fiesta Manjares, was one of the last of the Esselen Indian tribe, a small band whose ancient sites have been found in the upper Carmel Valley around Tularcitos and Tassajara. She married Luigi Piazzoni, a Swiss immigrant who had bought 6,000 acres in the Carmel Valley, and together they reared eight girls and a boy. One of the girls, Helen (above), stands by her horse at the Piazzoni Ranch. Another girl, Florence, married and reared her family a block from the high school in Monterey. Florence's daughter, Marie, was a cheerleader there, and sons Roy and Doug were outstanding varsity football players. Doug Forzani is seen around 1940 (left) on his pony outside the family home at Larkin and Madison Streets. (Courtesy Doug Forzani.)

Three Piazzoni sisters, Helen (left), Alice (center), and Edith are ready to rope at the ranch in the Carmel Valley. A fourth sister, Florence, was mother of footballer/cowboy Roy Forzani, whose own son was a career rodeo bullfighter. A fifth sister, Irene Piazzoni, born in 1892, raced in the Wild West Show at the first Salinas Rodeo in 1911 and rode in every parade for the next 60 years. (Courtesy Doug Forzani.)

Lou Hare was the first elected Monterey County supervisor and spent much of the 1912 Big Week in the arena at the Salinas Rodeo memorializing riders and animals with his camera. Here he himself was caught on film.

Photographer and surveyor Lou Hare split his time between the family home in Salinas, his ranch by the river in Chualar, and his rooms at the Casa Sanchez in downtown Monterey. Through his lens, one sees here the opening-day parade of the Salinas Rodeo in the photograph above, put on every third week of July, entering the rodeo grounds on what had been part of the old El Sausal Rancho. The rodeo has always attracted participants from far and wide but also has been a venue for Monterey County cowboys and cowgirls to showcase their talents. Below is Happy Jack Hawn and his wife—he a popular rider in the early days and she a trick roper.

The automated "machine" made its appearance in Monterey County just after the dawn of the 20th century, but for years afterward, horseback riding and the use of pack animals remained a way of life. Above is eight-year-old Dorothy Hare being taken camping in the summer of 1908 by McPhail, one of her father's ranch hands. The destination was Cachagua, deep in the Carmel Valley, and two serious grades had to be traversed. It was before the advent of sleeping bags, so a box spring was packed. At right is Dorothy Hare seven years later going into Cachagua again, this time with school friends and on horseback.

Thanks to its putative powers, the Tassajara Hot Springs attracted local Native American tribes for hundreds of years. It was not until 1890 that Chinese laborers completed a one-way road with hairpin turns blasted out of solid rock above a perpendicular wall dropping 3,500 feet in six miles. It would be another 22 years before it was open to automobiles. At left is a 15-year-old Dorothy Hare (left) with two high school friends about to ride down into Tassajara in 1914. Below is a group of Salinas teenagers seated atop the first motorcoach used specifically to transport passengers and mail into Tassajara on a daily basis.

RIDING

Bill Askew was born at the start of the 20th century near Fresno and came to Carmel in the 1920s as superintendent of public works. In his off-hours, he roped and branded at local ranches, and above he is seen roping at the arena at Frank DeAmaral's stables in Carmel Valley c. 1940. When Askew retired, his son took over his position with the City of Carmel and also did much of the branding in the area. Below, Bill Askew Jr. is shown in the late 1940s at a neighborly branding event at the San Carlos Ranch in lower Carmel Valley. The pickup truck serves as the chuckwagon. Pictured from left to right are Stuyvesant Fish, Leonard Rockwell, Ginny Fish, Askew, and Al Horner. (Both courtesy Bill Askew Jr.)

The Askew family tradition of working with horses and cattle has been carried forward by Bill Askew III and his sister Lynne Askew. As captain of the Hartnell College girls' rodeo team in Salinas, Lynne competed in Arizona, Nevada, and around California with her specialties being team and breakaway roping. Her brother is the livestock manager at Rana Creek Ranch, 20 miles inland from the coast in the Carmel Valley. He has also been part of winning team competitions throughout the state and has won individual figure-eight events. This photograph is of Bill Askew III in the arena at the Carmel Valley Trail and Saddle Club at Ranchero Days in 1999. His father, Bill Askew Jr., is coming through the gate. (Courtesy Bill Askew Jr.)

The Presidio of Monterey, so named by the War Department in 1904, became home to the 11th U.S. Cavalry Regiment in 1919. The 11th was organized in 1901 to take part in the Philippine insurrection, later participated in the Cuban pacification, and in 1916–1917 accompanied the punitive expedition into Mexico. When it came to the Presidio, the regiment's strength was at 26 officers and 661 enlisted men but underwent reorganization twice before it was transferred to border patrol in 1940 and then to Fort Benning, Georgia. There the horse cavalry became the 11th Armored Regiment. While at the Presidio, the troopers drilled their horses at Gigling Reservation (later Fort Ord). One of their training techniques for long rides involved the changing of mounts while underway. (Courtesy City of Monterey, Presidio of Monterey Museum.)

For the 21 years that the 11th Cavalry was at the Presidio in Monterey, it lent considerably to the social fabric of the area. Parades and ceremonies held at Soldier Field on the post were open to the public, as were boxing matches at the recreation center. Local youngsters were given the opportunity to exercise the horses, and girls from La Ida's and Flora Woods's establishments on Cannery Row would appear on Sundays in their finery and were not discouraged from riding. Troopers had two mounts each, which they drilled regularly. Above, a horse jumps over its rider, a confidence builder for both, and at left, trooper Marfa Tesas wins first prize on Ranger in 1929. (Both courtesy City of Monterey, Presidio of Monterey Museum.)

Polo had been played on the Monterey Peninsula since the Hotel Del Monte built a combination polo field, racetrack, and airstrip behind the present fairgrounds in 1896. Some 20 years later, the hotel and polo grounds came under the ownership of Sam Morse and his Del Monte Properties Company, and horsemanship came to the forefront on the peninsula. In February 1920, a "horseback field day" was held at the polo grounds, an event that included a steeplechase, a mounted tug-of-war, and a "corking good polo match." At the end of 1926, Morse wrote in *Game and Gossip*, which he published, "Del Monte has one of the foremost polo plants in the world," and the 1927 season was hugely successful. The legendary Tommy Hitchcock played for George Gordon Moore's Del Monte team, and a Major Erwin of the Presidio of Monterey fielded a strong side. One of the 11th Cavalry polo players is shown with his mallet and pony. (Courtesy City of Monterey, Presidio of Monterey Museum.)

The Del Monte Properties Company struggled through the Depression, and its recreational empire suffered the effects felt by the broader society. Polo reached its apogee on the peninsula in the late 1920s and then declined throughout the 1930s. Still, games continued to be held at the polo grounds until 1942, when the facility was leased by the military. Here a women's team is seen in action in 1940. (Courtesy Monterey Public Library, California History Room Archives.)

In 1941, Dick Collins became head of the Pebble Beach Equestrian Center, which Del Monte Properties Company constructed in the early 1920s. It held its first annual horse show and riding competition for children there in 1924, starting a tradition that Collins formalized in 1946 when he attracted 87 entrants. (Courtesy Mrs. Richard Collins.)

As director of the Pebble Beach Equestrian Center from 1940 to 1980, Dick Collins was known particularly for his training of young people in all phases of horsemanship. As well, he became a leader in sponsoring three-day "eventing," which is the core equestrian sport of the Olympic games. In eventing, the first day is given over to dressage, the second day to a cross-country steeplechase, and the final day to show jumping in an arena. Dick Collins was inducted into the Eventing Hall of Fame in 2003 and the polo field at the center bears his name. (Courtesy Mrs. Richard Collins.)

Across America, People are Discovering Something Wonderful. Their Heritage.

Arcadia Publishing is the leading local history publisher in the United States. With more than 3,000 titles in print and hundreds of new titles released every year, Arcadia has extensive specialized experience chronicling the history of communities and celebrating America's hidden stories, bringing to life the people, places, and events from the past. To discover the history of other communities across the nation, please visit:

www.arcadiapublishing.com

Customized search tools allow you to find regional history books about the town where you grew up, the cities where your friends and family live, the town where your parents met, or even that retirement spot you've been dreaming about.

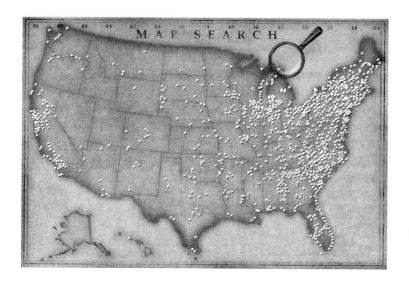